Victo

Victoria

Short Stay Guide

LITTLE HILLS PRESS

Text: Chris Baker, May 2003

Maps by MAPgraphics © Little Hills Press

Cover Design by Michael Brown
Edited and designed by Michael Brown

Printed in Singapore

Victoria
Short Stay Guide
ISBN 1 86315 2091

Little Hills Press
Sydney, Australia
◉www.littlehills.com
✎lhills@bigpond.net.au

Little Hills Press is a proud supporter of the See Australia National Tourism Initiative. See Australia is a Federal and State Government and Industry funded initiative launched in November 2000. Its purpose is to ensure Australians rediscover the importance of holidays (in particular Australian holidays) in maintaining a balanced life and to recharge the batteries in order to cope with the pace of life in the 21st century.

See Australia acknowledges and thanks its industry sponsors. Premium sponsors: Accor Asia Pacific (Hotel and Resorts Category), Mastercard International (Preferred Credit Card). Partners: AAA Tourism, Avis, Captain Cook Cruises, Hertz, lastminute.com, Qantas and travel.com.au

Please visit www.seeaustralia.com.au, the portal to all Australian travel and tourism information and product.

The use of See Australia's name and logo in this publication has been authorised by See Australia on the basis that the publisher has acknowledged and agreed to recognise See Australia's sponsors (above) without fee and and that those sponsors will not be disadvantaged commercially by the manner of the use of placement of See Australia's name, style or logo in this publication. See Australia does not expressly or impliedly endorse the products and services featured in this publication nor is it expressly or impliedly responsible for any representation made in this publication. To the extent permitted by the law, See Australia is not liable for any injury, damage or loss arising from the use or unavailability of any services or products featured in this publication or any representation made or not made in this publication.

DISCLAIMER

Whilst all care has been taken by the publisher and authors to ensure that the information is accurate and up to date, the publisher does not take responsibility for the information published herein or the consequences of its use. The recommendations are those of the writing team, and as things get better or worse, with places closing and others opening, some elements in the book may be inaccurate when you arrive. Please inform us of any discrepancies so that we can update subsequent editions.

Contents

Introduction
Acknowledgements 6
How to Use this Book 7

Regions
Melbourne 9
Lakes Entrance 37
Healesville and the Yarra Valley 45
Bright and the Victorian Alps 49
Shepparton 57
Bendigo 63
Echucha-Moama 69
Ballarat 75
Ararat and the Grampians 83
Mildura 89
Warrnambool and the Great Ocean Road 95
Geelong 103
Portland 107

Appendices and Indices
Victoria: An Overview 111
Australia: General Info 114
Travel Information 117
General Index 120
Budget Forms 128
Trip Log 130
Photo Log 131
Map Index 132

Acknowledgements

Thanks

A special thanks to the helpful staff at the following Tourism outlets for assisting with the production of this book:

Tourism Victoria, Alpine Region Tourism, Ballarat Tourism, Bendigo Tourism, Bright Visitors Centre, City of Melbourne, Geelong Tourism, Lakes & Wilderness Tourism, Lorne and Surfcoast Visitor Information Centre, Mildura Rural City Council, Phillip Island Visitor Information, Warrnambool Visitor Information, Yarra Valley Regional Tourism Association,

Maps

Maps supplied courtesy of MapGraphics

Photography

We are very grateful to Tourism Victoria for allowing us access to their library of excellent photographs.

Photographs courtesy of Tourism Victoria on pages 3, 5, 6, 7, 9, 14, 16, 17, 18, 19, 21, 23, 26, 27, 29, 30, 32, 33, 34, 36, 37, 38, 41, 43, 44, 45, 47, 49, 51, 52, 54, 55, 56, 57, 60, 61, 63, 66, 67, 68, 69, 72, 73, 74, 75, 79, 80, 82, 83, 86, 88, 89, 93, 95, 99, 101, 102, 103, 106, 107, 110, 111, 117, 119, 120 and 132.

Photographs courtesy of Leonardo on pages 11, 12 and 13

All other photographs supplied courtesy of Little Hills Press.

How to Use This Book

Symbols

Throughout the text you will find that symbols have been used to denote the information that follows, whether it be an admission price, opening time, phone number or web address. This will aid you in locating the specific details you desire more quickly.

Here is a list of the symbols used with an explanation of each:

- ℭ   indicates a phone number
- ✪   indicates a price
- ☺   indicates opening times
- 👁   indicates a web site
- ⚞   indicates an email address

Goods and Services Tax

The prices quoted in this book include Australia's 10% GST. It should also be kept in mind that many products are exempt from the tax, including basic food items.

Accommodation and Eating Out

The Accommodation and Eating Out sections contain by no means an exhaustive list of what Australia has to offer. We have tried to cater for a range of tastes and provide suggestions for your selection. They are designed to give you a basis for comparison and to act at the very least as a starting point for the planning of your holiday. All budgets from lavish to limited have been considered and included.

With regard to eating out, remember that there are always cheaper meals available at fast food outlets and in the food courts of most shopping complexes; we have focused on listing only popular and recommendable restaurants. Again, the GST is excluded from any prices listed. For ease of reference, these pages have been coloured differently:

Accommodation pages are yellow and **Eating Out** pages are purple

Layout

The chapters of this book are laid out by region, with the major population centres listed first. Information on chosen locations can be accessed easily, regardless of which direction you are heading, or what part of Victoria you cover.

From regional characteristics, how to get there, where to stay, and what to see, we have approached in detail every way a visitor might occupy his or her touring time, with the intention of helping to make the most of that limited time. The headings are clear for ease of use, and our comprehensive Index and Appendices will assist you in locating your area of interest.

We hope your stay in Victoria is both memorable and enjoyable.

Nagambie

Euroa

Longwood

Graytown

Hwy

Avenel

Mangalore

Puckapunyal

Seymour

Bonnie Doon

Merton

Strathbogie

Tatong

Violet Town

Cheshunt

King Valley

Mt Buffalo 1723 m

Bright

Mount Beauty

Mt Bogong 1986 m

Falls Creek

Mt Feathertop 1922 m

Glen Valley

Be

Mt Hotham 1862 m

Hotham Heights

Omeo

Mt Tabletop 1588 m

Dargo R

Goulburn

FRASER NP

Lake Eildon

Tolmie

Mansfield

Alexandra

Eildon

Hume

Broadford

Yea

Mt Buller 1804 m

Mount Buller

Mt Howitt 1742 m

Kilmore

Flowerdale

Taggerty

Jamieson

Mt McDonald 1625 m

ALPINE NP

Mitchell

Heathcote Junction

Buxton

Mt Kent 1563 m

Wallan

Glenburn

Gaffneys Creek

Whittlesea

Toolangi

Marysville

YARRA RANGES NP

Woods Point

Mt Tamboritha 1640 m

Dargo

Castleburn

Craigieburn

Healesville

Upper Yarra Reservoir

Aberfeldy

Licola

MITCHELL RIVER NATIONAL PARK

Bullumwa

Wiseleigh

Hurstbridge

Lake Thomson

MELBOURNE

Warburton

Yarra Junction

Avon

Walpa

River

Bairr

DANDENONG RANGES NP

Baw Baw

Mt Baw Baw 1563 m

Briagolong

104

Lake

Monbulk

BAW BAW NP

Newry

Maffra

Eagle Point

Emerald

Cockatoo

Above: North and East of Melbourne   *Below: South and West of Melbourne*

Lake Goldsmith

Cardigan

Wallace

Sunb

Mininera

Haddon

BALLARAT

Buninyong

Western

Gordon

Ballan

Myrniong

Diggers Rest

Snake Valley

Smythesdale

Scarsdale

Mt Egerton

Highway

Streatham

Glenelg

Highway

Linton

Newtown

Napoleons

Midland

Lal Lal

Bacchus Marsh

Rowsley

Melton

Skipton

Carranballac

Clarendon

Creek

Cape Clear

Elaine

BRISBANE RANGES NATIONAL PARK

MELBOURN

ura Pura

Lake Logan

Dereel

Corindhap

Meredith

Werribe

Rokewood Junction

Leigh

Moorabool

Rokewood

Anakie

Werribee

Derrinallum

Lismore

Werneth

Berrybank

Lethbridge

Little River

Princes

76

Werrib South

Darlington

Cressy

Shelford

Teesdale

Lara

Port P

Lake Gnarpurt

Lake Martin

Hamilton

River

Bannockburn

Corio Bay

Bay

Lake Bookar

Lake Corangamite

Inverleigh

Hwy

Batesford

GEELONG

Portarlington

Lake Colongulac

orat

Beeac

Lake Beeac

Mount Moriac

Barwon

22

Clifton Springs

Leopold

St Leo

rang

Camperdown

Warrion

Alvie

Winchelsea

Highway

Moriac

Lake Connewarre

Swan Isla

Coragulac

River

Modewarre

Ocean Grove

Queensc

Cobden

Cororooke

Lake Colac

Warncoort

Birregurra

Barwon Heads

Point Lonsdale

Pirron Yallock

Colac

Bellbrae

Breamlea

Torquay

Point Nepean

Melbourne

Population 2,942,000

Melbourne, the capital of Victoria, is situated on the shores of Port Phillip Bay. The Yarra River flows through the city.

Settlers in Van Diemen's Land (Tasmania) had known for years that there was good grazing land in the Port Phillip area, but had been refused permission to settle there. In 1835, John Batman ignored the ban, landed with a party, and 'bought' 600,000 acres of land from the local Aborigines for a few axes and other trade goods. He then returned to Launceston and formed the Port Phillip Association. (On the north side of Flinders Street, between Market and William Streets, there is a small plaque in the pavement marking the place where Batman stood when he declared that it was a good place for a village.)

In 1836, Governor Bourke vetoed Batman's purchase, and appointed Captain William Lonsdale as resident magistrate of the rap-idly-growing settlement. Bourke visited the site in the following year, named the place Melbourne, had a street plan drawn up, and offered lots for sale.

The Australian Colonies Government Act was passed in August 1850, and constituted the Port Phillip district as a separate colony, with La Trobe as its first Lieutenant-Governor. Soon after, gold was discovered near Ballarat, and people came from all over the world seeking fortune. The consequent Eureka Uprising gave the new government its first major challenge.

Climate

Melbourne's climate is midway between maritime and continental, and is very changeable. Average temperatures: January max 26C (79F) - min 14C (57F); July max 13C (55F) - min 6C (43F). Average annual rainfall: 656mm (26 ins). The driest months are June to August.

Melbourne

Victoria is called the Garden State, and its capital city certainly does its share to live up to that reputation. Melbourne has tree-lined boulevards, acres of parkland on the banks of the Yarra River, and parks and gardens galore in the suburbs.

How to Get There

By Air

Melbourne International Airport, at Tullamarine, is serviced by over 20 international carriers.

The domestic lines of Qantas ℂ 13 1313, and Virgin Blue ℂ 13 6789 , have regular services from other cities in Australia. Aus-Air, ℂ (03) 9580 6166, specialise in services to Tasmania and the southern islands of Flinders and King.

The airport is about 20km (12 miles) out of the city, and the Skybus operates between Tulla-marine and the terminal at 58 Franklin Street, ℂ 9335 3066 or ℂ 9662 9275. The Frankston & Peninsula Airport Shuttle, ℂ 9783 1199, takes passengers to that area, and there are shuttle buses for the eastern suburbs.

By Bus

Greyhound Pioneer/McCaffertys, ℂ 13 2030, have regular services to/from Melbourne and Sydney, Adelaide, Canberra, Newcastle, Coolangatta, Brisbane, Alice Springs, Townsville, Perth, Cairns and Darwin.

By Rail

There are rail services from Sydney and Adelaide, with connections from other capital cities, ℂ 13 2232. The country and interstate terminal is Spencer Street Station.

V/Line

Rail and coach services operate from country Victoria to Melbourne daily. They also travel as far as Adelaide, Canberra and the Sapphire Coast of NSW. For further information, ℂ 136 196.

By Road

From Sydney, via the Hume Highway, 875km (544 miles); via the Princes Highway, 1058km (657 miles); via the Olympic Way, 961km (597 miles); via Canberra/Cooma/Cann River, 1038km (645 miles).

From Adelaide, via the Western and Dukes Highways, 726km (451 miles); via Princes Highway West, 910km (565 miles).

Visitor Information

The Victoria Visitor Information Centre is in the Melbourne Town Hall on the corner of Swanston Walk & Little Collins Street, ℂ (03) 9658 9955. It is ◷ open Mon-Fri 8.30am-5.30pm and weekends and public holidays 9am-5pm. They can be emailed at the address: ✉ visitor@melbourne.vic.gov.au

There are information booths in Bourke Street Mall, between Elizabeth and Swanston Streets, and Flinders Street Station, on the corner of Flinders and Swanston Streets.

The Victorian Tourism Operators Association is on Level 2, Rialto North Tower, 525 Collins Street, ℂ (03) 9614 8877 or email ✉ vtoa@vtoa.asn.au

Tourism Victoria is on Level 6, 55 Collins Street, ℂ (03) 132 842.

City of Melbourne, is in Melbourne Town Hall, Swanston Street, ℂ (03) 9658 9955.

The Travellers' Aid Society of Victoria is on the 2nd Floor at 169 Swanston Street, ℂ (03) 9654 2600. They are ◷ open Mon-Fri 8am-6pm and Sat-Sun 10am-4pm. They also have a Rail Room at Spencer Street Railway Station, ℂ (03) 9670 2873.

Melbourne also has an Information Line available 7 days, from 8am-6pm - ℂ 13 28 42. The following websites will give you a detailed insight into the city of Melbourne, outlying regions and potential itineraries for travel around Victoria:

👁 melbourne.citysearch.com.au
👁 www.melbourne.org
👁 www.tourism.vic.gov.au
👁 www.theage.com.au
👁 www.victrip.vic.gov.au

Accommodation

For a complete list of accommodation, contact one of the Tourist Offices above or explore the web pages.

As with any big city, accommodation is usually cheaper in the outer suburbs, and that is obviously where you find the caravan parks.

Here is a selection of city and inner suburban accommodation, with prices for a double room per night, which should be used as a guide only. The telephone area code is 03.

Left: Hotel Sofitel, Middle and Right: Le Meridien at Rialto Melbourne

5-Star

Hotel Sofitel, 25 Collins Street, 9653 0000. 363 rooms, 52 suites, licensed restaurant, gym - $310-1760.

Le Meridien at Rialto Melbourne, 495 Collins Street, 9620 9111. 242 rooms, 10 suites, licensed restaurant, pool, spa, sauna, gym - $425-1030.

Hilton on the Park Melbourne, 192 Wellington Parade, East Melbourne, 9419 2000. 398 rooms, 38 suites, licensed restaurant, pool, spa, sauna, gym, barbecue - $300-430.

Grand Hyatt Melbourne, *(See Picture Overleaf)* cnr Exhibition & Lonsdale Streets, 9657 1234. 547 rooms, 26 suites, licensed restaurant, swimming pool, spa, sauna, gym, tennis - $270-630.

4-Star

Centra Melbourne, cnr Flinders & Spencer Streets, 9629 5111. 384 rooms, 13 suites, licensed restaurant, gym, heated swimming pool - $195-275.

Accommodation

The Grand Hyatt

Rydges Melbourne, 186 Exhibition Street, ⓒ9662 0511. 363 rooms, 70 suites, licensed restaurant, undercover parking, pool, sauna, spa, gym - ✪$195.

The Chifley on Flemington Melbourne, 5 Flemington Road, North Melbourne, ⓒ9329 9344. 227 rooms, 9 suites, licensed restaurant, bistro, pool, gym, sauna - ✪$135-200.

3-Star

The Batmans Hill Hotel, *(See Picture Opposite)* 66 Spencer Street, ⓒ9614 6344. 85 rooms, licensed restaurant, undercover parking - ✪$140-160.

Hotel Ibis, *(See Picture Opposite)* 21 Therry Street, ⓒ9639 1988. 250 rooms, licensed restaurant - ✪$110-190.

Kingsway Motel, cnr Park Street & Eastern Road, South Melbourne, ⓒ9699 2533. 40 units - ✪$115-135.

Treasury Motor Lodge, 179 Powlett Street, Melbourne, ⓒ94175281. 21 units- ✪$130-150.

Flagstaff City Motor Inn, 45 Dudley Street, West Melbourne, ⓒ9329 5788. 39 units, spa - ✪$110-160.

Marco Polo Inn, cnr Harker Street & Flemington Road, North Melbourne, ⓒ9329 1788. 70 units, licensed restaurant, swimming pool, sauna - ✪$110-200.

Hotel Enterprize, 44 Spencer Street, ⓒ9629 6991. 150 rooms, licensed restaurant - ✪$100.

2-Star

City Square Motel, 67 Swanston Street, ⓒ9654 7011. 24 units, basic facilities - ✪$105.

Melbourne Suburbs

Brunswick

Princes Park Motor Inn, 2 Sydney Road, ⓒ9388 1000. 70 units - ✪$125-135.

Parkville Motel, 759 Park Street, ⓒ9388 1500. 20 units - ✪$90.

Accommodation

The Hotel Ibis   Batman's Hill Hotel

Coburg

Coburg Motor Inn, 726 Sydney Road, Coburg North, ✆9350 1855. 26 units, swimming pool, undercover parking - ✪$85-95.

Coburg Coach Motel, 846 Sydney Road, Coburg North, ✆350 2844. 27 units, licensed restaurant (closed Sunday), swimming pool - ✪$75.

Footscray

Footscray Motor Inn, 90 Droop Street, ✆9687 6877. 30 units, licensed restaurant (closed Sunday) - ✪$120-155.

Mid Gate Motor Lodge, 76 Droop Street, ✆9689 2300. 25 units - ✪$85.

St Kilda

Cabana Court Motel, 46 Park Street, ✆9534 0771. 16 units, 16 suites - ✪$100-120.

Crest on Barkly Hotel Melbourne, 47 Barkly Street, ✆9537 1788. 60 units, sauna - ✪$110-160.

Serviced Apartments

South Yarra Place Apartments, 41 Margaret Street, South Yarra, ✆9867 6595. 18 studio apartments - ✪$70-165.

Caravan Parks

Melbourne Holiday Park, 265 Elizabeth Street, Coburg, ✆9354 3533. (No pets allowed), 120 sites, heated pool - powered sites ✪$23 for two, cabins $90-95 for two.

Ashley Gardens Holiday Village, 129 Ashley Street, Braybrook, ✆9318 6866. (No pets allowed) 106 sites, tennis, heated pool - powered sites ✪$23, cabins $70-100 for two.

Sylvan Caravan Park, 1780 Hume Highway, Campbellfield, ✆9357 0009. (No dogs or cats) 101 sites - powered sites ✪$20 for two.

Youth Hostel in 78 Howard Street, North Melbourne, ✆9329 8599. It has 34 rooms at ✪$25-35 per person twin share. Another is at 76 Chapman Street, North Melbourne, ✆9328 3595. It has 59 rooms at ✪$18 per person twin share.

A Melbourne Tram

Local Transport

The Met, Melbourne's public transport system, covers trains, trams and buses, and is operated by the Public Transport Corporation. Melbourne is divided into three zones and your ticket type depends on which zone you are going to travel in, and for how long. Two-hour, daily, weekly, monthly or yearly tickets are available.

The routes of the various forms of transport are indicated on the Met map, available from railway stations, newsagencies and some book shops. Further information is available from the Met Transport Information Centre, 589 Collins Street, ☎13 1638 (☼open 7am-9pm), or from The Met Shop at 103 Elizabeth Street.

Melbourne's metropolitan public transport website for Bayside Trains is ☞www.met.vic.gov.au

Victoria's official public transport site, containing timetables and fares for trams, buses and trains, is ☞www.victrip.com.au

Trams

Trams are just about the 'symbol' of Melbourne, and are a big draw-card for visitors. These vehicles, some old-fashioned and some sleek and new, continue to provide transport for thousands of commuters.

They are an interesting, reliable and efficient way to see the city. The Visitor Centres can provide you with a brochure outlining the routes, stops, zones and fares, with explanations to assist your reading of tickets (Metcards) and timetables.

Here are a few hints: remember to take coins with you, as this is the only form of currency which ticket vending machines accept. You can purchase a daily ticket for ✪$4.40, allowing you unlimited travel in Zone 1, which covers the city and immediate surrounds. Keep an eye out for retailers displaying the Metcard Sales Flag, because daily tickets must be pre-purchased. In the city centre, there is a free tram service, the Free City Circle, which skirts the rectangular perimeter of the CBD and may be useful for reducing your legwork while shopping or sightseeing.

Taxis

These can be hired off the street, at taxi ranks, major hotels, or by phoning one of the taxi companies.

Initial flagfall is ✪$2.60 and the meter clicks over at ✪$1 per kilometre, or at 41.6 cents per minute if the speed of the vehicle drops below 25km/h. There is a booking fee of $1 and also a late night surcharge of $1. Be aware that CityLink tolls will be added to the fare if you choose to travel on certain roads - both the Western and Southern Links are ✪$2 for taxis.

Following are some of the companies operating in Melbourne:
Arrow Taxi Service, ✆13 2211; Astoria Taxis, ✆9347 5511; Black Cabs Combined, ✆13 2227; Embassy Taxis, ✆13 1755; Frankston Radio Cabs, ✆9786 3322; North Suburban Taxis, ✆13 1119; Regal Corporate Cars, ✆9326 6600; Silver Top Taxi Service, ✆13 1008; West Suburban Taxi, ✆9689 1144; Yellow Cabs, ✆13 19 24.

Water taxis include:
River Yarra Water Taxis, ✆0416 06 8655; and Melbourne Circle Water Taxis, ✆9686 0914.

Car Hire

There are plenty of car rental agencies, and they accept current international licences.

Airport Rent A Car, ✆9335 3355; All Cheap Car Rentals, ✆9429 6999; Atlas, ✆9633 6233; Avis, ✆9330 4011; Budget, ✆1300 362 848; Crown, ✆9682 2266; Delta, ✆9330 6122; Europcar, ✆1300 131 390, Hertz, ✆13 3039; Murphy, ✆9602 2265; National, ✆9696 9000; Pacific, ✆9347 9600; Thrifty, ✆1300 367 2277.

When driving in Melbourne, there are a few rules about the trams. Drivers must not obstruct trams, and there are yellow lines on roadways indicating streets in which drivers must keep clear of the tracks when trams are approaching. Drivers must also stop when a tram is picking up or setting down passengers, if there is not a central traffic island. Making a right hand turn can sometimes be dicey in the city centre. If the intersection has a 'hook turn' sign, the turn has to be made from the left-hand lane when the lights change, to leave the centre of the intersection clear for trams.

Tollways

Citylink is a system of roads that connects some of Melbourne's motorways together. At the time of writing, Citylink tolls are applicable on the Monash Freeway, Tullamarine Freeway and the Bolte Bridge. No other motorways in Melbourne have tolls on them.

Leave your change in your pocket, though, because tolls are collected electronically. Most people visiting Melbourne will only want to use Citylink a couple of times at most. It is possible to buy up to twelve day passes per year on Citylink. Day passes cost ✪$3.85 and can be paid for with a Visa, Mastercard or Bankcard over the phone or bought at selected Shell service stations. Day passes can be bought up until 12pm the day after travel, but an extra fee for late day passes applies. The Citylink customer service number to pay for the pass is ✆13 26 29.

Bicycle Hire

Melbourne has quite a few bike tracks, and to hire a bike it is best to get in touch with Bicycle Victoria, 19 O'Connell Street, North Melbourne, ✆9328 3000.

Melbourne

Eating Out

Melbourne

Melbourne has over 3200 restaurants representing 70 national cuisines. The most plentiful choice of Asian restaurants is found in Chinatown's Little Bourke Street; for Italian food, try Lygon Street, Carlton; for Greek, Lonsdale Street; and for Vietnamese, Victoria Street, Richmond. South Yarra is another restaurant centre.

Here is a selection of highly recommended restaurants.

Asian

Flower Drum, 17 Market Lane, ©9662 3655. This is the number one Chinese restaurant, with a legendary status in Melbourne culinary circles. The question, however, is whether the justifiable fame, outstanding cuisine and impeccable service are worth the average $150 bill for two. The Drum is open for dinner 7 days and lunch Mon-Sat, licensed.

Mask of China, 117 Little Bourke Street, ©9662 2116. Licensed, excellent seafood and wine list, dinner served daily from 6pm, lunch on Sunday from midday.

Empress of China, 120 Little Bourke Street, ©9663 1833. Open for dinner 6 days and lunch on Sundays.

Bamboo House, 47 Little Bourke Street, ©9662 1565. Licensed. Peking duck and spicy seafoods are specialties. Open daily from 5.30pm and for lunch Mon-Fri.

King of Kings, 209 Russel Street, ©9663 2895. Inexpensive meals of a good quality, open daily 11am-2.30am.

Isthmus of Kra, 50 Park Street, South Melbourne, ©9690 3688. Gernerally considered one of the finest Thai restaurants in Melbourne. Licensed, wonderful wine list, varied menu, open for dinner 7 days and lunch Mon-Fri.

European

Austria Haus Edelweiss, 419 Spencer Street, ©9329 5877. Licensed, open 7 days for lunch

Lonsdale Street

Eating Out

Lygon Street

and dinner, with Viennese Sunday luncheon.

Casa Di Iorio, 141 Lygon Street, Carlton, ©9347 2670. Italian cuisine restaurant and pizza house, plus takeaway.

Da Salvatore, 29 Gratton Street, Carlton, ©9663 4778. Pizza, pasta and steaks, quick service, open 7 days for lunch and dinner.

Bonum, 2 Collins Street, City, ©9650 9387. Licensed, up-market restaurant with inventive and exotic dishes at prices around $25 for a main course. Open for dinner Mon-Sat and lunch Mon-Fri.

2bc, 177 Greville Street, Prahran, ©9529 4922. Busy and trendy establishment that serves Mediterranean-style meals at reasonable prices. It is licensed and open for lunch 7 days and dinner Mon-Sat.

Akvavit, Ground Level 3a, 2 Southgate, Southbank, ©9699 9947. Swedish restaurant with views of the river and city. Licensed or BYO, open daily for lunch and dinner. Two people can escape here paying around $40 for meals plus drinks.

International

O'Connels, 407 Coventry Street, South Melbourne, ©9699 9600. A changing menu that ranges from North American to Middle Eastern cuisine. Licensed, open for lunch and dinner 7 days.

Harvey's, 10 Murphy Street, South Yarra, ©9867 3605. Predominantly Asian and Italian flavours. Open daily for lunch and dinner, from 7am Mon-Fri.

Melbourne

Eating Out

Blakes, Ground Level, 2 Southgate, Southbank, ©9699 4100. Extensive menu offering a variety of unique flavours. Wonderful views of the Yarra and city. Open daily for lunch and dinner.

Becco, 11-25 Crossley Street, ©9663 3000. Efficient service, strong wine list and an extensive menu. Open daily 9am-11pm.

Chinois, 176 Toorak Road, South Yarra, ©9826 3388. Expensive but elegant modern restaurant. Licensed, open for lunch and dinner Mon-Fri.

Abla's, 109 Elgin Street, Carlton, ©9347 0006. Considered to be the best Middle Eastern restaurant in Melbourne. Set menu with a variety of complementary flavours. Open Thu-Fri for lunch and Mon-Sat for dinner.

est est est, 440 Clarendon Street, South Melbourne, ©9682 5688. Short but innovative menu with good wines to match. An expensive venture. Licensed and open Mon-Sat from 6pm.

Theatre Restaurants

Hofbrauhaus, 18-24 Market Lane, Melbourne, ©9663 3361. Bavarian beerfest. Affordable lunch menu. Licensed, open daily midday to midnight.

Dirty Dick's Medieval Madness Restaurant, 45 Dudley Street, West Melbourne, ©9325 3999. Licensed, medieval banquet.

The Comedy Club, 380 Lygon Street, Carlton, ©9348 1622. Open 9am-5pm Mon-Fri. Fully, licensed, cabaret environment, dinner and show packages available.

Witches in Britches, 84 Dudley Street, West Melbourne, ©9329 9850. Bar, three course meal and a two-hour show to follow. Open

Southbank

7pm-1am 7 days.

Dracula's Theatre Restaurant, 169 Exhibition Street, Melbourne, ©9663 1754. Comic Transylvanian theme. Centrally located in the city.

At the other end of the scale, KFC is at 201 Bourke Street and 37 Swanston Street. Pizza Hut is on the corner of Elizabeth and Bourke Streets (©13 1166 for delivery). There are no less than 11 McDonalds branches, with 4 on Bourke Street, 2 on Collins Street, 2 on Elizabeth Street, and one each on Lonsdale, Swanston and St Kilda. Of course, the suburbs are represented by additional branches of each of the above.

You will find many other types of fast food outlets in the city centre. Going hungry in Melbourne is almost impossible, except in cases when you remain indecisive for hours, overwhelmed by the wide choice of venues. But this seldom occurs.

Entertainment

Melbourne's nightlife conjures up images of excitement, colour, action and entertainment. There is a comprehensive range of nocturnal activities to select from including discos, wine bars, concerts, theatre, cinema, live bands, nightclubs and much more.

  Here is a selection of entertainment venues in the city.

Cinemas

Hoyts Cinema Complex, 140 Bourke Street, ℡9663 3303.

Village Centre, 206 Bourke Street, ℡9667 6565.

Chinatown Cinema, 200 Bourke Street, ℡9662 3465.

Crazy Horse Cinema, 34 Elizabeth Street, ℡9654 8796.

Greater Union, 131 Russell Street, ℡9654 8235.

Kino Cinemas, 45 Collins Street, ℡9650 2100.

Lumiere Cinemas, 108 Lonsdale Street, ℡9639 1055.

Moonlight Cinemas, Level 10, 140 Bourke Street, ℡9663 9555.

Theatres

The *Half-Tix* kiosk is in the Bourke Street Mall, ℡9650 9420.

Princes Theatre, 163 Spring Street, ℡9299 9800.

Victorian Arts Centre, 100 St Kilda Road, ℡9281 8000.

Athenaeum Theatre, 188 Collins Street, ℡9650 1500.

Comedy Theatre, 240 Exhibition Street, ℡9209 9000.

Playbox Theatre Company, 113 Sturt Street, South Melbourne, ℡9685 5111.

Melbourne Theatre Company, 129 Ferrars Street, Southbank, ℡13 6166.

Her Majesty's Theatre, 219 Exhibition Street, ℡9663 3211.

Forum Theatre, 154 Flinders Street, ℡9299 9700.

Princess Theatre, *(above)* 163 Spring Street, ℡9662 2911.

Regent Theatre, 191 Collins Street, ℡9299 9860.

Sidney Myer Music Bowl, Kings Domain, ℡9281 8360.

Nightclubs

Chevron, 519 St Kilda Road, ℡9510 1281. ⏲Open Thu 9pm-5am, Friday midnight-10am. Cover charge ✪$12.

Melbourne Metro, 20-30 Bourke Street, ℡9663 4288. ⏲Open Thu-Sat. Cover charge ✪$6 Thursday, $10 Friday & Saturday.

Revolver Upstairs, 229 Chapel Street, Prahran, ℡9521 5985. ⏲Open Mon-Thu midnight-3am, Fri-Sun 24hrs.

The Dome, 19 Commercial Road, Prahran, ℡9529 8966. ⏲Opens daily from 10pm with a cover charge of ✪$10.

Grainstore Tavern, 46 King Street, ℡9614 3570. Live acts upstairs, video dance club downstairs.

The Ivy, 145 Flinders Lane, ℡9650 1855. Open Thurs-Sat, four floors, dance, bar, band and VIP Bar upstairs.

Club V, 371 Chapel Street, South Yarra, ℡9827 1771. ✪$10 cover charge.

Salt, 14a Claremont Street, South Yarra, ℡9827 8333. One of Melbourne's most so-

Melbourne

phisticated nightclubs.

Billboard, 170 Russell Street, ✆9639 4000. ⏰Open Mon, Thurs-Sat 9pm-7am.

Club UK, 169 Exhibition Street, ✆9663 2075. Geared towards the backpacker sector - perhaps those who are feeling a little homesick. ⏰Open Wed-Sun 5pm-3am and there is no cover charge.

Monsoon's, in the Grand Hyatt Melbourne, 123 Collins Street, ✆9653 4516.

P O D, 241 King Street, ✆9642 8100. As the name indicates, this venue is quite simply a 'Place Of Dance'.

Chaise Lounge, 105 Queen Street, Melbourne, ✆9670 6120. Good music, plenty of seating, vibrant atmosphere and post-modern decor. ⏰Open from 4pm Tue, Wed & Fri and from 9am on Saturday, closing at 3am.

Bars & Pubs

Up Top Bar, First Floor, 163 Russell Street, ✆9663 8990. ⏰Open from 4pm until late the following morning Wed-Sun. Nostalgic '50s decor revised in trendy style. Impressive list of alcoholic beverages. Entry is free.

Gin Palace, 191 Little Collins Street, ✆9654 0533. Characterised by an eclectic mix of furniture fashions and cocktail concoctions (try an 'Industrial Revolution', for example!). ⏰Open daily 4pm-3am.

Hairy Canary, 212 Little Collins Street, ✆9654 2471. An inviting complement of food is on offer for those who feel that they need something to wash down with their drink. ⏰Open 7.30am-3am 7 days.

The Bullring, 95 Johnston Street, Fitzroy, ✆9416 0022. Lively atmosphere with music and dance of Latin American derivation. ⏰Open from 6pm-late, entertainment begins at 10.30pm. ◐$5 cover charge.

Walters Wine Bar, Upper Level, Southgate, Southbank, ✆9690 1211. Popular after-dark venue with stunning city views across the Yarra River. Good meals also available. ⏰Open midday every day and closes Sun-Thu at 1am and Fri-Sat at 3am.

Bell's Hotel, 157 Moray Street, South Melbourne, ✆9690 4511. Meals from 6pm.

Redback Brewery, 75 Flemington Road, North Melbourne, ✆9329 9400. ⏰Open Mon-Thurs 11am-midnight, Fri-Sat 11am-1am, Sun 11am-11.30pm. Meals Mon-Sun noon-3pm and 6-10pm.

Edward's Tavern, 221 High Street, Prahran, ✆9510 9897. 3 main bars and live entertainment. ⏰Open from 7pm Fri-Sun & Tues, 9pm Mon & Thurs, closed Wednesdays.

Music Venues

Rock

Wayside Inn, 466 City Road, South Melbourne, ✆9699 8469.

Central Club Hotel, 246 Victoria Street, North Melbourne, ✆9329 7482.

Jazz

Dizzy's Jazz Bar, 90 Swan Street, Richmond, ✆9428 1233. A deservedly famous centre for jazz lovers. ⏰Open Thu-Sat 8pm-1am. Cover charges are ◐$8 on Thursday and $10 on Friday & Saturday.

Moylans, 384 Flinders Lane, Melbourne, ✆9629 1030. Smoke-free environment, and a magnet for talented jazz musicians.

Ozcat, at the Parkview, cnr Scotchmer Street & Georges Road, Fitzroy North, ✆9489 8811. This venue will be used only for special concerts, while the main features of the Australian Catalog of Independent Artists will be played at Moylans (*see above*).

Rhythm & Blues

The Next Blue, at the Crown Casino, 8 Whiteman Street, South-bank, ✆9292 7007.

Shopping

Melbourne is Australia's fashion capital, and has an enormous selection of clothes and accessories boutiques.

Collins Street has many designer label boutiques, and is linked to Bourke Street by a network of arcades and alleys with boutiques and specialty shops. Explore the sidewalks

Melbourne Central Shopping Complex

along Collins Street between Swanston and Spring Streets for some exclusive up-market clothing stores.

234 Collins, located at that address, is a complex dedicated to fashion.

Australia on Collins is another fashion mecca. It joins Collins and Little Collins Streets and boasts an elaborate food court.

The 19th century *Block Arcade*, with its high domed ceiling and mosaic tiled floor, runs from 282 Collins Street to Little Collins Street, or you can enter from Elizabeth Street.

The *Royal Arcade*, the oldest arcade in Melbourne, links Little Collins Street and Bourke Street Mall, and also has an entrance in Elizabeth Street.

For a more modern feel, you could try the enormous *Central Shopping Complex*, which features an enormous glass cone on the top of its building (the largest free standing glass structure of its type in the world). It is opposite Myer and extends from Lonsdale through to La Trobe Streets. The *Galleria Plaza* is a centre for fashion and also a good place to find gifts. It is on the corner of Elizabeth and Little Collins Streets.

The *Bourke Street Mall* in the heart of the city, between Swanston and Elizabeth Streets, offers very good shopping, and is dominated by David Jones and Myer Department Stores. Other arcades running off the Mall are the **Centrepoint Mall** and **The Walk**. Although the Mall is classed as a pedestrian area, trams do run through its centre.

Midtown Plaza is on the corner of Bourke & Swanston Streets.

If you are searching for **duty free** shopping, head to the stretch of Elizabeth Street between Bourke and Lonsdale Streets.

The bazaar-like character of: the **Queen Victoria Market**, cnr Victoria and Elizabeth Streets; the **Prahran Markets**, Commercial Road, just off Chapel Street; **South Melbourne Markets**, York Street, off Ferrars Street; and the **Victorian Arts Centre Sunday Markets**, 100 St Kilda Road, South Melbourne, each offer an alternative and entertaining shopping experience.

Toorak Village, in Toorak Road from Punt Road to Williams Road has restaurants, boutiques and expensive furniture stores.

A little further out in Campbellfield at 400 Mahoneys Road, just off the Hume Highway, is the **Pipeworks Fun Market**, ©9357 1155, with 600 shopping stalls, fun rides, live entertainment, mini-golf and bungee jumping.

Many **shopping tours** are available to factory outlets. Here are a few of the options:

Shopping Spree Tours, 2/77 Asling Street, Gardenvale, ©9596 6600. 8.30am-5pm daily, ✪$50 a head.

Special Buying Tours, 198 Cotham Road, Kew, ©9817 5985. 9am-5pm Mon-Sat, ✪$15-40 a head.

Melbourne Shopping Tours, 7 Almeida Crescent, South Yarra, ©9826 3722.

Points of Interest

City Explorer Bus. Taking a tour on the City Explorer Bus is a good way to get your bearings. This red and white double-decker leaves from Swanston Street, just outside the Visitor Information Centre, on the hour between ⊙10am-4pm and visits most of the main city attractions with its 16 stops. There are discounts on entry into nominated venues and other perks that might appeal. The costs are ✪$22 adults, $10 children and $50 for families. For additional infor-mation, ©9650 7000. Enquire also about the evening City Lights Tour or the Half-Day Tours which include Australian Wildlife, Shrine of Remembrance & Botanical Gardens and All Around Melbourne.

Melbourne Museum. The Melbourne Museum replaced the Museum of Victoria, formerly in Swanston Street, which is now closed as a result. This $263 million project places Victoria's newest museum to the north of the Royal Exhibition Building in Carlton Gardens, off Nicholson Street. Its exhibits focus on the natural environment and new technologies. Among the many facilities are an Aboriginal Centre, a Forest Gallery, a Mind and Body Gallery, Technology Exhibitions and a Science Gallery, ©8341 7777. Adults ✪$12, children $5, families $30. Apart from the attractive garden surrounds, an **IMAX Theatre**, off Rathdowne Street, opened on the site in 1998, ©9663 5454. The nearby **Royal Exhibition Building**, built in 1880, is itself worth a visit for its history and architecture, ©9270 5000 for enquiries.

Immigration Museum. The museum is located in Old Customs House, on the corner of 400 Flinders Street and William Street, ©9927 2700. This musuem takes visitors through a cultural tour using interactive computer displays and permanent physical exhibits. Personal stories are recounted by immigrants themselves, providing insights into the emotions and memories of immigration experiences. The museum is ⊙open between 10am and 5pm and admission is ✪$7 adults, $5.50 concession, $3.50 children and $20 for families. The best method of transport is the Free City Circle tram, which passes nearby on Flinders St between 10am and 6pm.

Hellenic Antiquities Museum. Located on the second floor of Old Customs House, this museum is designed to host periodical exhibits of ancient Grecian and Byzantine treasures, and is a joint venture of the Victorian and Greek governments. It shares opening times and entry fees with the Immigration Museum on the ground floor, ☏9927 2700 for current and upcoming showcases.

Scienceworks Museum. Science-works is a short 10 minute drive from the city centre, and occupies the futuristic cylindrical building in 2 Booker Street, Spots-wood, which cannot be missed. Exhibitions include a detailed exploration of the human body and its mechanics (*Stayin' Alive*), and a 'behind-the-scenes' look at producing special effects for movies and television (*The Sequel*). Also included in the complex is the fascinating Melbourne Planetarium. Admission is ✪$8 adults, $6 concession and $4 children, and the museum is ⊕open 10am-4.30pm, ☏9392 4800 for more details.

State Library. The oldest public library in Australia, established in 1856, is on the corner of Swanston and La Trobe Streets. It contains over one million books and periodicals, as well as overseas manuscripts, maps, microfilms, a multimedia catalogue, paintings and photographs. The La Trobe Library is located in a special wing opened in 1965. It is ⊕open Mon-Thurs 10am-9pm, Fri-Sun 10am-6pm, ☏9669 9888.

Rialto Towers. An excursion to the top of Rialto Towers, 525 Collins Street, ☏9629 8222, is absolutely imperative for any visitor. The magnificent panoramic vista, completely unobstructed from mountain to ocean and everything in between, is undoubtedly the best way to see Melbourne and its surrounds. At 253m in height, it is the tallest office building in the Southern hemisphere. The Observation Deck is accessible ⊕Sun-Thu 10am-10pm and Fri-Sat 10am-11pm, adults ✪$7, children $5.

State Library

Old Melbourne Gaol. The National Trust has preserved one remaining cell block as a penal museum, which has a unique collection tracing the story of transportation, convicts, and the development of Victoria's penal system. It is believed that 104 hangings were carried out at the gaol, including that of Ned

MELBOURNE

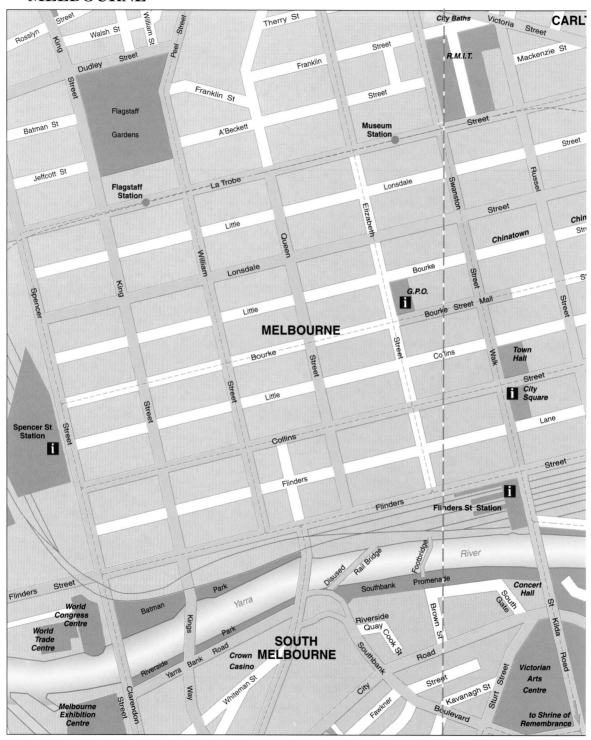

CARL
City Baths   Victoria   Street
Therry St
Rosslyn   Street
Walsh St
King
William St
Peel   Street
Franklin
Street
Mackenzie St
R.M.I.T.
Dudley   Street
Franklin
Street
Street
Batman St
Flagstaff
Franklin St
A'Beckett
Museum
Station
Street
Gardens
Street
Jeffcott St
La Trobe
Lonsdale
Swanston
Street
Flagstaff
Station
Elizabeth
Little
Russel
Street
Chin
Str
William
Queen
Chinatown
Lonsdale
Bourke
Spencer
King
G.P.O.
Street
Bourke   Street   Mall
S
Little
MELBOURNE
Street
Street
Town
Hall
Bourke
Street
Colins
Walk
Street
Little
Street
City
Square
Spencer St
Station
Lane
Street
Collins
Street
Flinders
Flinders
Flinders St Station
River
Flinders   Street
Disused   Rail Bridge
Footbridge
World
Congress
Centre
Park
Yarra
Southbank   Promenade
Concert
Hall
Batman
South
Gate
Brown St
World
Trade
Centre
Kings
Park
Road
Riverside
Quay
Cook St
St Kilda   Road
Riverside
Yarra   Bank   Road
Crown
Casino
SOUTH
MELBOURNE
Southbank
Road
Victorian
Arts
Centre
Clarendon
Street
Whiteman St
City
Street
Sturt   Street
Melbourne
Exhibition
Centre
Way
Fawkner
Kavanagh St
Boulevard
to Shrine of
Remembrance

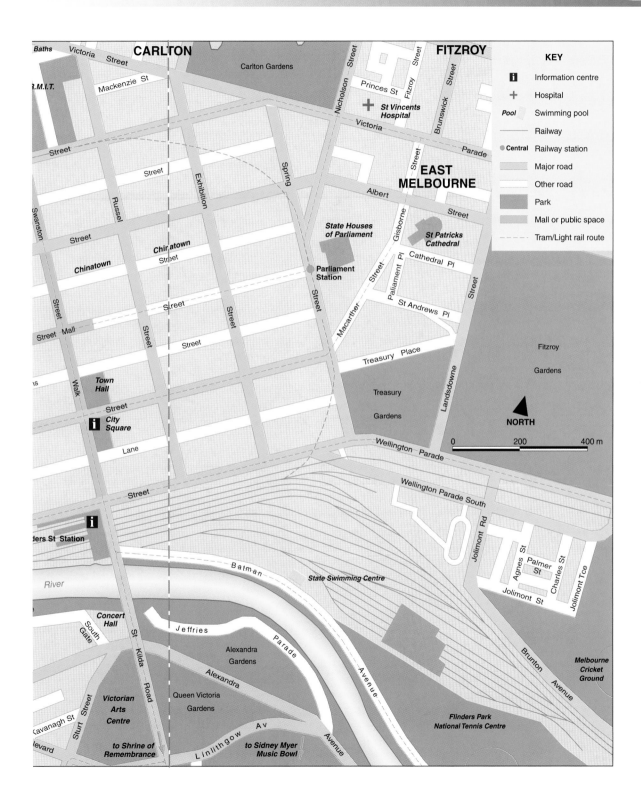

CARLTON

FITZROY

KEY

Baths | Victoria | Street

Mackenzie St

R.M.I.T.

Carlton Gardens

Nicholson Street

Princes St | Fitzroy Street

Brunswick Street

St Vincents Hospital

Victoria | Parade

EAST MELBOURNE

Street | Street

Exhibition

Spring

Albert | Street

Swanston | Russel | Street

Chinatown | Street

Chinatown

State Houses of Parliament

Gisborne

St Patricks Cathedral

Street | Street | Street | Street

Street | Mall

Parliament Station

Macarthur | Street

Parliament Pl | Cathedral Pl

St Andrews Pl

Walk

Town Hall

Treasury Place

Fitzroy Gardens

City Square

Treasury Gardens

Landsdowne

Lane

Wellington Parade

NORTH

0   200   400 m

Street

Wellington Parade South

Flinders St Station

Jolimont Rd

Agnes St | Palmer St | Charles St | Jolimont Tce

River

Batman

State Swimming Centre

Jolimont St

Concert Hall

South Gate

St Kilda Road

Jeffries

Parade

Brunton Avenue

Melbourne Cricket Ground

Victorian Arts Centre

Alexandra Gardens

Alexandra

Queen Victoria Gardens

Avenue

Flinders Park National Tennis Centre

Kavanagh St | Sturt Street

to Shrine of Remembrance

Linlithgow

Av

to Sidney Myer Music Bowl

Avenue

KEY

- **i** — Information centre
- **+** — Hospital
- *Pool* — Swimming pool
- —— Railway
- ● **Central** — Railway station
- Major road
- Other road
- Park
- Mall or public space
- – – – Tram/Light rail route

Chinatown

day-4.30pm, Sun-Fri 10am-4.30pm, and entry fees are ❂$5 adult and $3 concession, ✆9662 2888.

Fire Services Museum Victoria. The museum, on the corner of 39 Gisborne Street and Victoria Parade, East Melbourne, was once the Eastern Hill Fire Station. Now it has displays of restored fire fighting equipment used by fire brigades throughout the city. The museum is ⏲open Fri 9am-3pm, Sun 10am-4pm, with admission ❂$5 adults, $2 children and $10 for families, ✆9662 2907.

Parliament House. The State Houses of Parliament in Spring Street, at the top of Bourke Street, were built in stages between 1856 and 1930, and have never actually been finished as the dome and facades to the side and rear were never added. Guided tours of this Victorian construction are available at 10am, 2pm and 3pm Mon-Fri when Parliament is in recess, ✆9651 8911.

The Old Treasury. This fine public building was restored, converted to a museum and reopened in 1994. It is situated in Spring Street, at the top of Collins Street, ✆9651 2233. There are three permanent exhibitions which encompass the past history and contemporary life of the city, its art, culture and architecture. The layout of the museum is designed for self-guiding, but guided tours are offered at 1pm and 3pm. The Treasury is ⏲open 9am-5pm Mon-Fri and 10am-4pm on weekends and public holidays. Admission is ❂$5 adults, $3 children and $13 for families.

St Patrick's Cathedral. This Gothic Revival cathedral is in 1 Cathedral Place, which runs off Lansdowne Street, East Melbourne, and is constructed of Footscray bluestone. It was completed in 1897, except for the spires, which were added in 1936. There is a statue in the churchyard of the great Irish liberator, Daniel O'Connell, which is a replica of that which stands in O'Connell Street, Dublin. The Cathedral contains many beautiful works of art and it is ⏲open from 9am-5pm Mon-Fri, ✆9662 2233.

Kelly on November 11, 1880. The gaol is located in Russell Street, near Victoria Street, and ⏲opens daily 9.30am-4.30pm, with admission ❂$9 adults, $6 children and $25 for families, ✆9663 7228. For ❂$15 adults, $8 children and $39 families, shows are conducted on Wednesday and Sunday nights - but some may consider them to be suggestively violent in nature, so be warned if you plan to take young children.

Chinatown. Chinatown is in Little Bourke Street, and extends from Exhibition Street to Swanston Street. It contains many restaurants from the most economical to the extremely expensive. The **Chinese Museum** is in 22 Cohen Place, and is one of the best small museums in Melbourne. It is ⏲open Sat mid-

Federation Square

Federation Square is the first major city project to break Melbourne's traditional rectangular grid pattern, joining the CBD to the Yarra river. This complex series of structures, the winner of an international design competition, is located on the intersection of Flinders Street and Swanston Street.

Fitzroy Gardens. Bounded by Albert, Clarendon, Lansdowne Streets and Wellington Parade in East Melbourne, Fitzroy Gardens are delightful nineteenth century gardens. The gardens contain **Cooks' Cottage**, ✆9419 4677, which was transported to Australia in 1934 and rebuilt block by block. It was originally built in the mid-eighteenth century by Captain James Cook's father. The cottage is ◷open daily 9am-5pm. Also in the garden are the famous Fairy Tree and the miniature Tudor Village replica. Next to Fitzroy Gardens are the **Treasury Gardens** containing the John F Kennedy Memorial.

Australian Gallery of Sport & Olympic Museum. The museum is outside the member's entrance to the **Melbourne Cricket Ground** in Yarra Park, Jolimont, and is Australia's first multi-sport museum. The three level building has priceless collections of memorabilia, which are displayed graphically in exhibitions aimed at entertaining and educating. The Australian Gallery of Sport now incorporates the Olympic Museum, which traces the history of the Olympics, from the ancient Greek games to the Modern Summer Olympics from 1896-1992. The museum is ◷open daily 10am-4pm, ✆9657 8879. For tours of the adjoining MCG, which depart every day on the hour between 10am and 3pm, ✆9657 8879.

Queen Victoria Gardens and Kings Domain. These were originally the site of a goldrush shanty-town, and were proclaimed public parkland in 1854. The area contains Australian and English trees, and one of the most attractive sections of the Kings Domain is a garden of rockeries, tiny paths and waterfalls which commemorate the Pioneer Women of Victoria. The **Myer Music Bowl**, ✆9281 8360, venue for many of Melbourne's most popular entertainment events, is in the Kings Domain.

The **Shrine of Remembrance**, also in Kings Domain, is dedicated to the sacrifice made by Victorian men and women in the two World Wars. A feature is the Stone of Remembrance, the centre of which is illuminated by a shaft of sunlight at exactly 11am on Armistice Day, November 11 each year. It is hopen every day between 10am and 5pm. There is no charge, but a donation box is located out the front if you wish to support the volunteers who give their time to conduct tours and answer your questions. For more information, ✆9654 8415.

The well-known **Floral Clock**, whose floral design is changed four times a year requiring the planting of over 30,000 flowers, is in the Queen Victoria Gardens.

La Trobe's Cottage. The Cottage, on the corner of Birdwood Road and Dallas Brooks Drive, in the Domain, South Yarra, was the colony's first Government House. La Trobe brought the house with him in the ship *Fergusson*, along with his family and possessions. The National Trust supervised the re-creation of the buildings, and they contain many of the original furnishings. The Cottage is ⏱open 11am-4pm Mon, Wed, Sat & Sun, ✆9654 4711.

Victorian Arts Centre Complex. On the banks of the Yarra River, at 100 St Kilda Road, the Centre comprises the theatres, the Melbourne Concert Hall, the Performing Arts Museum and the National Gallery of Victoria. As well as the performance and exhibition spaces, the Victorian Arts Centre has several restaurants. The **George Adams Gallery** has an extensive collection and is ⏱open Mon-Sat 9am-11pm, and Sun 10am-5pm, ✆9281 8194. The **Performing Arts Museum** has regularly changing exhibitions, free entry and is ⏱open Mon-Sat 9am-11pm, Sun 10am-5pm, ✆9281 8000. Guided tours of the Centre are available at limited times, ✆9281 8198.

Princes Bridge. The bridge is Melbourne's oldest and grandest, and is located at the point where Swanston Street becomes St Kilda Road. It was built around 1886, replacing a wooden bridge that had been opened by La Trobe in 1850.

Young & Jackson's Hotel. Also known as Princes Bridge Hotel, the pub is at 1 Swanston Street, ✆9650 3884. Its claim to fame is that the upstairs lounge is home to the infamous painting 'Chloe' which caused a scandalized public outcry when it was first hung in the Melbourne Art Gallery in the 1880s. She may have caused a stir then, but now she hardly manages to raise an eyebrow.

St Paul's Cathedral. This Gothic Revival Anglican cathedral is on the corner of Swanston and Flinders Streets, on the site of the first official church service in Melbourne. The Cathedral was completed in 1891, and the spires added between 1926 and 1931. The doors are ⏱open Mon-Fri 9am-5pm, ✆9650 3791.

Capitol Theatre. The astonishing ceiling of the theatre, at 113 Swanston Street, was designed by Walter Burley Griffin, the architect of the city of Canberra. Entry is ❂$8 adults, $4 children, ✆9654 4422.

Melbourne Town Hall. The Town Hall, in Swanston Street Walk, ✆9658 9779, was built between 1867 and 1870, and the portico added in 1887. It is worth going inside the main hall to see the chandeliers, murals and organ and the rest of its recenty restored interior. The Town Hall was one of the main venues for concerts before the advent of the Concert Hall in St Kilda Road.

Polly Woodside Maritime Museum. The barque *Polly Woodside*, in Lorimer Street East, Southbank, is a deepwater, square-rigged, commercial sailing ship built of riveted iron in 1885. Seventy years ago, she was one of the fast fleet of windjammers, today she is fully restored and is the centrepiece of a display of Australia's maritime history. ⏱Open 7 days 10am-4pm, admission ❂$7 adults, $4 concession and $15 for families, ✆9699 9760.

Melbourne Exhibition and Events Centre. At 28 Clarendon Street, South Melbourne, ✆9205 6400, this complex is the largest and most modern of its kind that Australia has to offer, and plays host to a wide range of exhibitions throughout the year. Its unique exterior design is worth a glance.

Crown Entertainment Complex. The complex is often described as 'the city under one roof', and indeed its restaurants, theatres, cinemas, Crown Towers Hotel, bars, nightclubs, showrooms, cocktail lounges, cafes, ballrooms, shopping boutiques and unabated gambling opportunities at the **Crown Casino**, do give the impression of a mini metropolis. The complex is in Southbank, and the Casino is at 8 Whiteman Street, ✆9292 8888.

Melbourne Aquarium. This Aquarium, situated on the corner of King Street and Queenswharf Road, City, ✆9620 0999, is a very sophisticated and impressive way to view ocean creatures. It has the enormous Oceanarium viewing tank, modern computer interactions, aquatic feeding facilities and a simulator. The complex is ⊙open daily 9am-6pm (until 9pm during summer), and costs adults ✪$17.50, concession $12.50 and children $8.50.

Suburban Attractions

Royal Botanic Gardens. The Royal Botanic Gardens are in Birdwood Avenue, South Yarra, and have 41ha (101 acres) of lawns, gardens and ornamental lakes. The Gardens are regarded as one of the finest examples of landscape gardening in the world. Their development commenced in 1846 under the direction of the then Superintendent of the Colony, Charles Joseph La Trobe, and now features 12,000 plant species. Brochures are available on special seasonal walks through the Gardens. **Como House**, Como Park, is an elegant colonial mansion, built in 1847, which has been classified by the National Trust and is ⊙open for inspection daily 10am-5pm, ✆9827 2500.

St Kilda

St Kilda is Melbourne's equivalent of Sydney's Kings Cross, only more so. Developers would like to move in and restore the area to the fashionable and wealthy resort it once was, but they are meeting resistance from long-established residents. From Swanston Street, there are many trams that run to St Kilda, including Tram 16 from Swanston Street, and from Bourke Street, Tram 96 goes through South Melbourne to St Kilda. From Richmond,

Luna Park

take Tram 79, which travels along Church Street, and Chapel Street in Prahran, then continues on to St Kilda Esplanade. By road, St Kilda is reached by the West Gate Freeway from the west, Punt Road from the north. **The Esplanade** runs along the beach, which is not very inviting, and leads to the St Kilda Pier, which has a kiosk built in 1904 at the corner. The St Kilda hot sea baths are nearby, and are very popular. **Luna Park** is in 18 Lower Esplanade, next door to the Palais Theatre, and has been run as a fun palace since the 1920s. There is a restaurant behind the Palais that was originally a bathing shed. Rides such as

Flemington Spring Carnival

the Mad Mouse, the Ghost Train and the Scenic Railway have been entertaining young ones for years. Entry is free into the Park but rides are priced at around ✪$2 or $3. It ⊙opens 11am daily and closes at 5pm Mon-Thu & Sun and 11pm Fri-Sat. **Rippon Lea**, 192 Hotham Street, Elsternwick, is a brick mansion built between 1868 and 1887, and has 33 rooms, iron carriage gates and a conservatory. It is set in a beautiful garden with a lake, and is one of the National Trust's pride and joys. It is ⊙open Tues-Sun 10am-5pm, ✆9523 6095. **Ripponlea Railway Station** is a fine example of early twentieth century architectural style.

Parkville

Parkville is a student area with colleges, halls of residence and student flats set amidst fashionable homes, office buildings and Victorian terraces. Its main attractions are the Melbourne Zoo and the nearby University of Melbourne.

The **Melbourne Zoo** is in Elliot Park, ✆9285 9300. It has a lion park, walk-through aviary and native fauna park, and a butterfly enclosure. More than 350 species are represented here in Australia's longest-standing zoo (since 1862). The *Lakeside Restaurant* serves 'meals with a view', looking out to Gibbon Island. Standard opening times are ⊙daily 9am-5pm, but some exhibits and special events have alternative times. It is recommended that you allow at least four hours to fully appreciate this attraction, and you can phone the above number for feeding times and other points of interest to better plan your visit. Admission is adults ✪$14.50, children $7.20 and $39.30 for families.

The **University of Melbourne**, Gratton Street, ✆9344 4000, dates back to the 1850s, and contains, among other interesting buildings, **The Grainger Museum**, Gate 13, Royal Parade, ✆9344 4270, which is ⊙open Mon 10am-1pm, Tue 10am-4pm and Wed-Fri 10am-4pm.

Flemington

Flemington Racecourse is one of the most beautiful courses in the world, and is worth a visit even if you are not into betting. Unfortunately, it is only open to the public on race days, but the crowds add to the atmosphere anyway. The daily papers have details of race meetings in the sports pages. The famous Melbourne Cup is run here on the first Tuesday of November.

Tours

The Visitor Information Centre has details of all tours that are available in and around Melbourne. Here are some examples.

Melbourne Discovery Pass
Duration: ◷12pm-5pm daily.
Attractions: Lunch at Rialto Towers, cruise on the *Melba Star* past Southbank and the Royal Botanic Gardens, Como Historic House, afternoon tea and return.
Cost: ✪$45
Operator: Rialto Towers Observation Deck, ✆9629 8222.

City Tour
Duration: ◷9am-12pm daily.
Attractions: City, Chinatown, Parliament House, Fitzroy Gardens, Captain Cook's Cottage, Melbourne Cricket Ground, National Tennis Centre, Albert Park, Westgate Bridge, Botanic Gardens, Shrine of Remembrance and return. Cost: ✪$45.
Operator: Gray Line, ✆9663 4455.

Melbourne Highlights
Duration: ◷1.30pm-5.30pm daily
Attractions: City, Chinatown, Shrine of Remembrance, South Yarra, Toorak, Dandenong Ranges, Sher-brooke Forest, Mt Dandenong and return.
Cost: ✪$46.
Operator: Gray Line, ✆9663 4455.

Best of Melbourne
Duration: ◷12.15pm-7.15pm daily
Attractions: Same as Melbourne Highlights but with the addition of dinner on the Colonial Tramcar Restaurant, which tours Melbourne streets at night while you eat.
Cost: ✪$122.
Operator: Gray Line, ✆9663 4455.

Penguin Parade and Seal Rocks
Duration: ◷Fluctuates with season, daily.
Attractions: Phillip Island by coach, Koala Conservation Centre, dinner at Cowes (price not included), viewing of Penguin Parade, Seal Rocks Seal Life Centre and return.
Cost: ✪$106.
Operator: Gray Line, ✆9663 4455.

Penguin Express
Duration: ◷5.30-11.30 daily between March and November.
Attractions: Express coach to penguin viewing on Phillip Island then return. Cost: ✪$72.
Operator: Gray Line, 9663 4455.

Melbourne's Best Tours
Duration: ◷Seasonal (late afternoon until late)
Attractions: Hotel pick-up in Melbourne, South Gippsland, Western Port Bay, Australian Wildlife, San Remo, tour of Phillip Island, Seal Rocks, Mutton Bird, Penguin Parade and return. Cost: ✪$75.
Operator: Melbourne's Best Tours, ✆1300 130 550.

Blue Dandenongs
Duration: ◷8.40am-5.30pm daily.
Attractions: Dandenong Ranges, Puffing Billy train ride, lunch at Fergusson's Winery, Healsville Sanctuary and return. Cost: ✪$112
Operator: Gray Line, ✆9663 4455.

Sovereign Hill
Duration: ◷9am-5.30pm daily.
Attractions: Coach to Ballarat, Sovereign Hill Historical Park, gold panning, provincial town tour and return. Cost: ✪$90
Operator: Gray Line, ✆9663 4455.

Winery Tour - Yarra Valley
Duration: ◷8.30am-5pm daily.
Attractions: 3-6 wineries, lunch, Badger Weir Park and return. Cost: ✪$118
Operator: Victorian Winery Tours, ✆9653 9749.

Additional tours of the Great Ocean Road, Grampians, Murray River and extended trips to Phillip Island are also available, and the Visitor Information Centre will supply you with details of all of them.

The Yarra River

The **National Trust (Victoria)** produces a brochure which you can pick up at the Visitor Information Centre. It outlines buildings of particular historical significance and includes all the relevant details for visiting them.

Apart from their regular city service, the **City Explorer Bus** offers a number of different tours in the Melbourne area and to outlying regions, ©9650 7000 to enquire further.

Cruises on the Yarra are also available. Here are companies which operate such services:

Melbourne River Cruises, Vault 18, Banana Alley Jetty, ©9614 1215.

City River Cruises, 3 Princes Walk, Melbourne, ©9650 2214.

Southgate River Tours, Southgate, Southbank, ©9682 5711.

Festivals

The Moomba Festival is held in March each year.

A parade is held before the Grand Final of the AFL competition in September.

The Melbourne Cup is held on the first Tuesday in November each year.

Sporting Facilities

Melbourne has four venues for horseracing - Flemington, ©9258 4666; Caulfield in Station Street, ©9257 7200; Moonee Valley in McPherson Street, Moonee Ponds, ©9373 2222; and Sandown in Racecourse Drive, Springvale, ©9546 9511.

An Australian Rules Football Match at the MCG

In summer, many International Tests, one day International and Sheffield Shield Cricket matches are played at the Melbourne Cricket Ground (MCG), Yarra Park, Jolimont.

There are two major venues for greyhound racing - Melbourne Park on Monday nights and Sandown Park on Thursday nights.

Harness Racing's main venue is Moonee Valley in Moonee Ponds, and races are held every Saturday and some Mondays.

Australian Rules Football (AFL) is played every Saturday during the season (March to September) at various grounds around the city, including the MCG.

Soccer's main venue is Melbourne Park, Swan Street, Melbourne, ✆9286 1600.

The Australian Tennis Open is held each year at the National Tennis Centre in Batman Avenue, East Melbourne, ✆9286 1600.

Calder Park Thunderdome, Calder Highway, Keilor, is Australia's only super speedway. For information on race meetings, ✆9217 8800.

The Australian Motorcycle Grand Prix is held at the Phillip Island Motor Racing Circuit, Back Beach Road, ✆5952 9400.

The Formula One Grand Prix is held at Albert Park in March, ✆9258 7100 for more information.

Melbourne has facilities for every type of sport, and venues and clubs are listed in the Yellow Pages telephone directory.

Penguin Parade, Phillip Island

Outlying Attractions

Phillip Island

Phillip Island is 129km (80 miles) from Melbourne, and is the home of the fairy penguins. At dusk, the famous penguins emerge from the surf, completely ignoring the thousands of curious onlookers. The Island has a Phillip Island Nature Park, which is divided into a number of outlets for wildlife viewing and information, including koalas, fur seals, pelicans, mutton birds, and the famous fairy penguins.

There are more than fifty places to stay in Cowes alone, the main tourist centre of Phillip Island. The districts of Newhaven, Rhyll and San Remo offer several alternatives. All types of accommodation are available.

The **Penguin Parade Visitors Centre**, off Ventnor Road, ©5956 8300, is open daily from 10am and you can view the seasonal nightly pilgrimage of the cute creatures as they waddle their way onto the beach and up the sand dunes. It costs adults ✪$11.50, children $6 and families $29.

The Koala Conservation Centre is located at Fiveways on Phillip Island Road, ©5952 1307. It ⊙opens at 10am, 7 days a week and costs ✪$5 for adults, $2 for children and $12 for families.

Churchill Island, accessed via Newhaven, off Phillip Island Road, is popular for its tranquil gardens and stunning array of bird life. Costs are ✪$5 adults, $2 children and $12 for families.

The Seal Rocks Life Centre, Penguin Reserve, The Nobbies, ℰ9793 6767, has amazing educational displays and panoramic views. Entry is ✪$10 adults, $5 children and $28 for families.

A *Four Park Pass* gives access to all four attractions listed above for the one price: ✪$25 adults, $12 children and $65 for families.

At the **Australian Dairy Centre**, Phillip Island Road, Newhaven, there is a museum explaining the history of the dairying industry, and a cheese factory with sales section and tastings. The cafeteria sells dairy-based light meals and snacks, ℰ5956 7583.

Other attractions include great surfing beaches and restaurants.

French Island National Park, which can be reached by ferry either from Cowes at Phillip Island or from Stoney Point on the Mornington Peninsula, is larger than Phillip Island although less developed.

In Korumburra, on the South Gippsland Highway east of Phillip Island, is **Coal Creek Heritage Village**, a re-creation of an 1890s coal mining/railway town, with 40 buildings, including a mine, blacksmith, printer, stores, and a saw mill, ℰ5655 1811.

For more information on Phillip Island attractions, contact the Phillip Island Information Centre, ℰ5956 7447, or drop into their outlet at Newhaven on Phillip Island Tourist Road. It is ⏱open 7 days a week, 9am-5pm.

You can take advantage of the comprehensive web page at ☞www.phillipisland.net.au, or the Centre's accommodation booking service on ℰ1300 366 422. Contact them via email at ✉info@ phillipisland.net.au

Another good website for planning and attractions details is ☞www.penguins.org.au which includes an email form at ☞www. penguins.org.au/trip/index.html

Tynong

Tynong is a town on the Princes Highway, on the way to Melbourne from Sale.

Here you will find **Victoria's Farm Shed**, Australia's leading farm animal theatre featuring parades, milking, shearing and sheep dog displays. Show times are 10.30am and 2pm daily. For more information, ℰ5629 2840.

Also at Tynong is **Gumbuya Recreation and Leisure Park**, a 174ha (430 acres) recreation park with toboggan slide, minicars, pony coach and trail rides, mini golf, playground, water slide, half court tennis, bbq and picnic areas, and a restaurant, ℰ5629 2613. The park is ⏱open every day 10am-6pm (rides in operation 11am-4pm) and admission is ✪$6 adults, $3.50 children and $19 for families.

Bass

Bass is located on the Bass Highway, on the way to Phillip Island from Melbourne.

The Giant Worm Museum, on the Bass Highway, is a unique attraction and education facility. They do actually have giant worms (including one you can walk through!), and many other historical and hands-on displays, ℰ5678 2222.

Mornington Peninsula

The Nepean Highway follows the eastern shore of Port Phillip Bay for 97km (60 miles) to the seaside resort of Portsea. On the way it passes picturesque peninsula beaches such as Dromana, Rosebud and Sorrento.

At Dromana, the **Arthur's Seat Scenic Chairlift** ride offers great views of Melbourne, Port Phillip Bay and the Mornington Peninsula. It ⏱opens at 11am daily September-April, and only on weekends and holidays during winter, ℰ5987 2565.

The MV *Peninsula Princess*, a car assenger ferry, operates every day linking the Mornington and Bellarine Peninsulas, from Queens-cliff to Sorrento.

Ashcombe Maze, Red Hill Road, Shoreham, ℰ5989 8387, is a large hedge maze believed to be the only significant one of its type in Australia. There are tea rooms surrounded by

Emerald Lake, Dandenong Ranges

extensive gardens. It is ⊙open from 10 am every day and costs ✪$6 adults, $4 children.

The Visitor Information Centre for Peninsula Tourism is at 359B Point Nepean Road, Dromana, ✆5978 3078. For web information 👁www. melbourne.citysearch.com.au includes the Mornington Peninsula region.

Dandenong Ranges

The Dandenongs are only 35km (22 miles) east of Melbourne, and the area is ideal for picnics, bushwalks and wildlife observation. It is an extremely popular destination with Melbournians and tourists for both daytrips and weekend escapes. Mt Dandenong (630m - 2067 ft) offers a panoramic view of Melbourne from its strategic lookout points.

One of the most popular attractions is Puffing Billy, Old Monbulk Road, Belgrave, ✆9754 6800, an historic narrow gauge train that runs through 13km (8 miles) of mountain scenery between Belgrave and Lakeside (Emerald Lake) in the Dandenong Ranges every day of the year, except Christmas Day. Return fares are adults ✪$17.50, children $9 and $49 for families. The line opened in 1900, and it is the ideal way to view the Dandenongs at close range. The suburban trains from all stations connect with Puffing Billy at Belgrave, one hour's easy drive from Melbourne.

The famous **William Ricketts Sanctuary**, Mt Dandenong Tourist Road, ✆13 1963, is set in the lush surrounds of the Dandenong Ranges and comprises the inspired sculptures of one artist. Encap-sulating the spirituality of Aboriginal culture and expressing an affinity with nature, these startling images bear a powerful mystique. The Sanctuary is ⊙open daily 10am-4pm and entry is ✪$5 adults, $2 children and $12 for families.

The Dandenongs are covered in 👁www.melbourne.citysearch.com.au

Lakes Entrance

Population 4,600
Lakes Entrance is the gateway to Gippsland Lakes, Australia's largest inland water system. It is 360km (224 miles) east of Melbourne, 840km (522 miles) south of Sydney and 429km (267 miles) south-west of Canberra.

Climate

Lakes Entrance has a temperate climate. The average maximum temperature in summer is 33C (91F), in winter 21C (70F). There is some rain in July and August, and occasional overnight showers in summer.

Characteristics

The largest town on Ninety Mile Beach, Lakes Entrance is a popular holiday destination. It has a spectacular hinterland with mountains (snow in winter), rivers and forests. Wildlife in the area includes dolphins and water birds, kangaroos, wombats, koalas and bush birds.

How to Get There

By Bus
Greyhound Pioneer, ✆13 2030, provides interstate connections.

By Rail
V/Line, ✆13 6196, offer a road and rail combination to Lakes Entrance.

By Road
Access is via Princes Highway from Melbourne and Sydney, and the Cann Valley Highway from Canberra.

By Air
Flying is not the preferred method of access to this area, but regional connections can be made throughout the district and the Visitor Information Centre will be able to advise on timetables and routes to suit your itinerary.

Visitor Information

The Lakes Entrance Visitor Information Centre is on the corner of Marine Parade and The Esplanade, ☏(03) 5155 1966. They are ⏱open 9am-5pm daily. Contact them on the internet at ✉ lakes@lakesandwilderness.com.au or simply explore the web page at 👁www.lakesandwilderness.com.au

Accommodation

As mentioned, Lakes Entrance is a popular holiday spot, so there is plenty of accommodation from which to choose, in fact over 60 places in the town. The Information Centre has a complete list, but here are a few examples with prices for a double room per night, which should be used as a guide only. The telephone area code is 03.

Banjo Paterson Motor Inn, 131 Esplanade, 5155 2933. 22 units, licensed restaurant, heated swimming pool, barbecue - ✪$115-190.

Abel Tasman Motor Lodge, 643 Esplanade, 5155 1655. 11 units, heated swimming pool, barbecue - ✪$70-165.

Golden Beach Motor Inn, 607 Esplanade, 5155 1666. 29 units, swimming pool, unlicensed restaurant - ✪$55-100.

Lakes Central Hotel, 321-333 Esplanade, 5155 1977. 16 units, licensed bistro, swimming pool, spa, barbecue - ✪$55-95.

Albatross Motel, 661 Esplanade, 5155 1779. 8 units, heated swimming pool, barbecue - ✪$50-135.

Lakeside Motel, 164 Marine Parade, 5155 1811. 27 units - ✪$45-90.

The Esplanade Motel, 251 Esplanade, 5155 1933. 40 units, car wash, heated swimming pool, spa, barbecue - ✪$40-125.

Lakes Seaview Motel, 12 New Street, 5155 1318. 11 units, barbecue - ✪$40-80.

Caravan Parks

Silver Sands Tourist Park, 33 Myer Street, 5155 2343. (No pets allowed) 37 sites, spa, pool, barbecue - powered sites ✪$18-30 for two, on-site vans $30-80 for two.

Riviera Country Caravan Park, 29 Palmers Road, 5155 1236. (No pets allowed) 62 sites, barbecue - powered sites ✪$17-26 for two, on-site vans $35-70 for two, cabins $40-90 for two.

Echo Beach Caravan Park, 33 Roadknight Street, 5155 2238. (Pets allowed under control) 25 sites - powered sites ✪$18-32 for two, cabins $45-110 for two.

Lakes Haven Caravan Park & Flats, 3 Jemmeson Street, 5155 2254. (No pets allowed) 17 sites, barbecue - powered sites ✪$17-28 for two, cabins $40-85 for two, holiday flats $45-105 for two, on-site vans $30-65 for two.

Lakes Entrance Tourist Park, 127 Princes Highway, 5155 1159. (Pets by arrangement) 100 sites, barbecue, heated pool - powered sites ✪$18-30 for two, cabins $35-95 for two. There is a **Youth Hostel**, ***Riviera Backpackers***, in 5 Clarkes Road, Lakes Entrance, 5155 2444. It has 19 rooms at ✪$15 per person twin share.

Festivals

Here are a few of the major events in the area:
January - the Metung Regatta, and the New Year's Eve fireworks at Lakes Entrance.
February - the Canni Creek Races near Buchan, the Cattlemen's Cup (every year in the high country, once every four years at Omeo).

March - the Marlay Point Overnight Yacht Race and the Bairnsdale Festival.
Easter - Rodeos at Omeo and Buchan, the Kinkuna Festival and Blessing of the Fleet at Lakes Entrance.
June - the Wildtrek at Dinner Plain.
November - the Flat Water Classic (windsurfing) at Paynesville.

Lakes Entrance

Lakes Entrance

Eating Out

There is the usual range of takeaway outlets, and most hotels serve counter meals. Local seafood is often the specialty on the menu. Some of the motels have restaurants, but here are the addresses and phone numbers of other restaurants you might like to patronise.

For a special dining experience try *Nautilus Floating Dockside*, Western Boat Harbour, The Esplanade, ℂ5155 1400. It is licensed, has a seafood specialty, and boasts an outstanding waterside location with views. This award-winning restaurant is open Mon-Sat from 6pm for dinner.

Egidio's Wood Oven, 573 The Esplanade, ℂ5155 1411. Licensed, Italian menu.

Ocean Dragon, 601 The Esplanade, ℂ5155 1349. Chinese cuisine.

Tres Amigos, 521 The Esplanade, ℂ5155 2215. Authentic Mexican flavours.

Shang Hai Garden, 215 The Esplanade, ℂ5155 2602.

Skippers, 481 The Esplanade, ℂ5155 3551.

The Scallop Pot, 221 The Esplanade, ℂ5155 1555.

Miriams, Shop 2, Level 1, 3 Bulmer Street, ℂ5155 3999.

Cafe Pelicano, 171 The Esplanade, ℂ5155 2166.

Pinocchio Inn, 569 The Esplanade, ℂ5155 2565.

McDonalds is at 359 The Esplanade. Although there are no KFC or Pizza Hut branches here, you will find an abundance of alternative fast food outlets along The Esplanade.

Points of Interest

The artificial entrance of the lakes to the ocean was completed in 1889, and there are still visible signs of the equipment used to bring logs and rocks from inland for the construction.

A short walk across the footbridge brings you to the Entrance and Bass Strait, with **Ninety Mile Beach** stretching away into the distance. A section of the beach is patrolled by the Surf Lifesaving Club during the holidays.

Nyerimilang Park on Lake King, Kalimna West Road, Nungurner, overlooks Rigby, Fraser and Flannagan Islands. It has bullock driving demonstrations and field days, and there are bushwalks, as well as barbecue and picnic facilities, ℂ5156 3253. Nyerimilang is Aboriginal for Chain of Lakes.

Kinkuna Country Fun Park & Zoo, Princes Highway, ℂ5155 3000 has waterslides, a toboggan ride with electronic timing, kiosk, souvenirs, crafts and games room. It is ☉open daily from 10am (weather permitting) and the entry fee includes barbecues, toddlers' pool, the jumping castle and wildlife area. The lions are hand-fed (not fed hands) at about 1pm on most days. Entry is ✪$4.50 adults, $4 children and toddlers under three are free.

Griffiths' Sea Shell Museum and Marine Display, 125 Esplanade, ℂ5155 1538, also has a gift shop and a model railway display. Over 90,000 shells from around the world are featured, and there is also a model railway room for locomotive enthusists. The complex is ☉open daily.

The Lakes Entrance Aboriginal Art & Crafts, 239 The Esplanade, ℂ5155 3302, has genuine Aboriginal artifacts on display and for sale. ☉Open 9am-5pm daily.

Ninety Mile Beach

Mansfield • Mt Tableto 1588 m • Omeo • Bindi • Mt Nunniong 1615 m • Mt Bowen 1320 m • Craigie • SE FOREST NATIONAL PARK

Mt Buller 1804 m • Mount Buller • Mt Howitt 1742 m • Swifts Creek • Gelantipy • Bonang • Bendoc • MT IMLAY NP • BEN B NP

Jamieson • Mt McDonald 1625 m ALPINE NP • Ensay • Murrindal • SNOWY RIVER NATIONAL PARK • ERRINUNDRA NATIONAL PARK • Buldah • Wonboyn L 162 • COOPRACAMBRA NATIONAL PARK

Gaffneys Creek • Mt Kent 1563 m • Dargo • Buchan • Combienbar • Noorinbee • Genoa

Woods Point • Mt Tamboritha 1640 m • Castleburn • Buchan South • Club Terrace • ALFRED NP • Mallaco

Licola • Buchan • MITCHELL RIVER NATIONAL PARK • Bullumwaal • Wairewa • Orbost 136 • Cann River • CROAJINGOLONG NATIONAL PARK

Yarra oir • Aberfeldy • Lake Thomson • Wiseleigh • Bruthen • Nowa Nowa • Newmerella • Cabbage Tree Creek • Bemm River

Baw • Mt Baw Baw 1563 m • Walpa • Briagolong 104 • Bairnsdale • Marlo

BAW BAW NP • Newry • Eagle Point • Lake King • Lake Tyers • Lakes Entrance

Walhalla • Maffra • Stratford • Paynesville

Moondarra • Heyfield • Lake Victoria

Willow Grove • Toongabbie • Loch Sport • Lake Wellington

Moe • Yallourn North • Sale • Longford • Paradise Beach

Traralgon • Golden Beach

Morwell • Churchill

Mirboo North • Carrajung • Seaspray

gatha • Wonwron • Jack Smith Lake

Lakes Entrance

Facilities

Boat cruises from Lakes Entrance, Metung, Lake Tyers, Paynesville. Sail and motor boat hire, daily or longer term, from Lakes Entrance, Metung, Paynesville, Lake Tyers, Johnstonville. Fishing from jetties, shoreline, from hired boats, or on organised fishing trips. Swimming in lakes and sea. Viewing the hot pools at Metung. Rafting and canoeing on rivers. Horse-riding - full day and extended trail rides. 4WD tours, bushwalking, tennis, lawn bowls, golf.

The Visitor Information Centre has all the information on times and locations, ✆(03) 5155 1966.

Outlying Attractions

Mallacoota

Reached via Genoa on the NSW/Vic border, Mallacoota is surrounded by the Croajinolong National Park. Mallacoota is situated in one of Victoria's most remote and peaceful lakeland settings. There are many walking tracks through the **Croajinolong National Park**, which has prolific birdlife.

If you wish to explore the natural wonders here, contact the Park Office, Genoa Road, Mallacoota, ✆(03) 5158 0263 or the Information Centre in nearby Cann River, ✆(03) 5158 6351.

Orbost

Orbost is the railhead for East Gippsland, and is situated on the Snowy River 16km from the coast. It is the gateway to Marlo where the Snowy meets the Brodribb River and where a sandbar allows the rivers to reach the sea. Scenic drives and walks are the main attraction of this stunning region. Cape Conran, reached via Marlo, has camping, picnic and walking facilities.

For ideas on the best places and routes to explore, the Snowy River Visitor Centre in Lochiel Street can be contacted on ✆(03) 5154 2424 or can be emailed at the address: ✉ orbost@ lakesandwilderness.com.au

Omeo

Omeo is on the way to the snowfields at Mt Hotham, about one-and-a-half hours drive from Bairnsdale. The town's history lies in timber, gold and cattle, and the town is like the backdrop for a movie set in the 1880s. Omeo is an ideal place to stop for a meal and to hire skis and chains during winter, and even close enough to stay in the town and visit the snow of Alpine National Park daily. Many people visit Omeo for trout fishing, bushwalking and canoeing.

Buchan

In the foothills of Snowy River Country, 56km (35 miles) from Lakes Entrance, lies the town of Buchan which is probably best known for its limestone caves.

The **limestone caves** were discovered in 1907, and the reserve surrounding them has picnic facilities, barbecues, and lots of kangaroos. There is also a swimming pool fed by an extremely cool underground stream. The rangers conduct tours through the caves during the day.

The Visitor Centre in Lakes Entrance produces a very good pamphlet detailing activities and attractions in the area, including a comprehensive driving map, ✆5155 1966.

Nowa Nowa

Situated approximately 24km (15 miles) from Lakes Entrance, Nowa Nowa is predominately a timber milling town. Numerous forest drives off the Princes Highway lead to delightful barbecue spots. Close by are the trestle bridge and the Mundic Creek waterfall at **Cosstick Weir**. The arm from **Lake Tyers** extends to the town, offering good fishing.

Gippsland

In general terms, the Gippsland area stretches from the east of Bairnsdale to Phillip Island, and north of Morwell and Traralgon down to Wilsons Promontory and Ninety Mile Beach on the southern coast, taking in just about everything in between. It covers the beautiful landscapes of fertile countryside and is full of various natural wonders from mountains and forests to rivers and beaches.

The best way to explore the Gippsland is by driving and the Visitor Centres can provide you with a range of material about the eight uniquely-themed drives listed below.

1. **Gippsland Heritage Track** - museums, historic buildings, shipwrecks, gold mines, antique shops and more.

2. **Walhalla and Mountain Rivers Trail** - Long Tunnel Extended Mine, Walhalla Cemetery, Stringers Creek Gorge, Walhalla Goldfields Railway.

3. **Wildlife Coast Nature Track** - Victoria's south coast including Phillip Island, National Parks, Ninety Mile Beach, walking trails, Wilsons Promontory.

4. **The Grand Ridge Road** - Strzelecki Ranges, rainforest and bushwakling areas.

5. **The High Country Adventure** - a journey through mountainous peaks providing breathaking views of rugged valleys below.

6. **The Country Road** - Great Dividing Range Hinterland, rural country, charming pubs, Alpine National Park.

7. **Gourmet Traveller Track** - sampling seafood, meat products, dairy selections, fresh vegetables and fine wines cultivated in the prosperous Gippsland soil.

8. **Power Track** - traces the history of coal mining in the region and takes you past the massive power generation facilities of the LaTrobe Valley.

Two information outlets are:

Gippsland Country Tourism Information Centre, Shop 1, Southside Central, Princes Highway, Traralgon, ☎ 5174 3199 or ☎ 1800 621 409 (toll free).

South Gippsland Visitor Information Centre, cnr South Gippsland Highway & Silkstone Road, Korum-burra, ☎ 5655 2233 or ☎ 1800 630 704 (toll free).

For more online information visit the website: 👁 www.gippslandtourism.com.au or email ✉ information@gippsland tourism.com.au

Lakes Entrance

Lakes Entrance

Paynesville

Known as the boating capital of the Gippsland Lakes, Paynesville *(pictured above)* is 18km (11 miles) south-east of Bairnsdale, with a well-marked turn off the Princes Highway. McMillan Strait, Newlands Arm and canals provide sheltered moorings for many pleasure and commercial fishing boats.

From Paynesville there are many places to go by boat - the **Lakes National Park**, with its picnic grounds and kangaroos, the beautiful **Duck Arm**, and three of Victoria's best **bream rivers**: Mitchell, Nicholson and Tambo. There is also a ferry that runs from Paynesville to **Raymond Island**, which is inhabited by kangaroos, koalas and water and bush birds.

Bairnsdale

Bairnsdale, just over 30km west of Lakes Entrance, was the port for its pastoral hinterland in the days before road transport. Now it supports a number of secondary industries. **St Mary's Roman Catholic Church**, ☎5152 2942, built in 1913 and extended in 1937, has unique murals by Frank Floreani, an incredible painted ceiling and other works of art.

The **Court House**, built in 1893 and classified by the National Trust, has delightful architecture, but it can only be viewed from the street.

The Historical Museum, Macarthur Street, has some interesting memorabilia on display,

☎5152 6363. It is ☉open Wednesday, Thursday and Sunday 1-5pm.

The Tourist Information Centre is at 240 Main Street, ☎(03) 5152 3444, and they have brochures and details of all attractions. You can email them at ✉ bairnsdale@ lakesandwilderness.com.au

Eagle Point

Eagle Point is only 15 kilometres, following the coastline south then east, from Bairnsdale. The well known Mitchell River silt jetties are found at Eagle Point. Eagle Point is also known for its fishing, both in Lake King and the Mitchell River.

Sale

Situated on the Melbourne side of Lakes Entrance, Sale is the operations centre for the nearby Bass Strait oil fields of Esso-BHP. There is also a large RAAF training base located here.

Cullinen Park, off Foster Street, is the site of the historic Port of Sale where, in days of yore, steamers tied up after their long trip from Melbourne. From Sale there are roads leading to the southern end of Ninety Mile Beach.

Apart from the historical interest of the town centre, including the **Gippsland Art Gallery** (68 Foster Street, ☎5142 3372) and the **Historical Museum** (Foster Street, ☎5144 5994), Sale is surrounded by attractive natural areas which include a **Wildlife Refuge** and the **David Morass State Game Reserve**.

The Central Gippsland Visitor Information Centre can be found in 8 Foster Street, ☎(03) 5144 1108. Email ✉toursale@i-o.net.au

Stratford

Stratford is a town located on the Avon River 17km north of Sale. A **Shakespearean Festival** is held here in April every year. For more details, ☎(03) 5145 6133, email ✉ dmccubb@netspace.net.au or visit the website at 👁home. bicnet.au\~shakes

Healesville & The Yarra Valley

Population 8,150
Healesville is 62km (38 miles) east of Melbourne, in the foothills of the Great Dividing Range.

Climate

The climate can be brisk in winter, with snow on the higher peaks.

Characteristics

Healesville is the gateway to towering ash forests, waterfalls and fern bowers. The township is surrounded by high mountains, and one of Victoria's most picturesque mountain highways climbs from Healesville to Marysville over the Black Spur through forests of mountain ash, beech and wattle.

How to Get There

By Rail
From Melbourne's Flinders Street Station, take a train to Lilydale, which connects with a V/Line coach to Healesville.

By Road
From Melbourne, via the Maroon-dah Highway.

Tourist Information

The Yarra Valley Visitor Information Centre is in The Old Courthouse, Harker Street, ℰ(03) 5962 2600, email ✉ info@yarravalleytourism. asn.au, or visit the site online at ☞www.yarra valleytourism.asn.au

Healesville

Accommodation

Healesville offers some accommodation, and here is a selection, with prices for a double room per night which should be used as a guide only. The telephone area code is 03.

Healesville Motor Inn, 45 Maroondah Highway, 5962 5188. 14 units, bbq - ✪$75-140.

Healesville Maroondah View Motel, 1 McKenzie Ave, 5962 4154. 10 units, unlicensed restaurant, pool - ✪$70-75.

Sanctuary House Healesville (Motel), 326 Badger Creek Road, 5962 5188. 12 units, restaurant, pool, spa, sauna - ✪$65-80.

Yarra Gables Motel, 55 Maroon-dah Hwy, 5962 1323. 5 units (private facilities) - ✪$99-140.

Caravan Parks

Badger Creek Caravan & Holiday Park, 419 Don Road, 5962 4328. (No pets) - powered sites ✪$20-24 for two, no on-site vans.

Ashgrove Tourist Park & Holiday Units, 322 Don Road, 5962 4398. (Pets allowed by prior arrangement) - powered sites ✪$20-22 for two, no on-site vans.

Eating Out

Some of the motels have BYO restaurants, and the hotels have licensed restaurants or bistros. Here are a few others you might like to try.

Mount Rael Restaurant, Healesville/Yarra Glen Road, 5962 4107 - BYO, Australian cuisine.

Strathvea Country House, Myers Creek Road, 5962 4109 - BYO, Australian cuisine.

Ming Gardens Restaurant, 271 Maroondah Highway, 5962 5067

Montiverdi Pizza Restaurant, 335 Maroondah Highway, 5962 4455 - BYO and licensed, eat in or takeaway.

Healesville Piquant Palate, 278 Maroondah Highway, 5962 3625, is a deli and restaurant. They specialise in Teddy Bears Picnic Baskets, specially prepared for a relaxing day in the country. They ask if orders for the baskets could be placed the day before they are needed.

Points of Interest

Hedgend Maze, at 163 Albert Road, is a giant hedge carved into a maze, with cryptic messages to solve on the way to help you get through. The grounds make for a pleasant picnic setting. It is open daily from 10am, 5962 3636.

Maroondah Reservoir is a popular place, and is set in a landscaped park of exotic and native trees, shrubs and flowers.

Badger Weir and **Donnelly's Weir** also provide beautiful bushland walks and superb picnic-barbecue areas. For the more energetic, walking tracks explore local National Parks and Forests.

Queen's Park, in the centre of the township, is ideal for picnics, and has a sports oval, tennis courts, children's playground and swimming pool.

One of the most popular attractions is the **Healesville Sanctuary** in Badger Creek Road, 5957 2800. The sanctuary is the only place where the platypus has been bred in captivity, and they are on display here between 11.30am-3.30pm. There are also koalas, wombats, kangaroos and emus, and a Nocturnal House with some of Australia's least-seen animals such as the Leadbeater possum, kowari, sugar gliders and potaroos.

The Reptile House has a selection of Australia's venomous snakes, and in another area there are lyrebirds, that have also been successfully bred here. The Sanctuary has a catering centre for picnic lunches, a licensed bistro, and a gift shop. ◷Open daily 9am-5pm.

11km (7 miles) west of Healesville is the township of **Yarra Glen**, and the Yarra Valley Tourist Railway winds between the two towns. A group of volunteers are in the process of making the railway a premier tourist attraction. Trolley rides can be taken from Healesville Station through a 100m old, brick-lined tunnel. Just out of Yarra Glen is the historic Gulf Station, which is worth a visit.

Toolangi, about 30km (19 miles) north of Healesville, was the home of C.J. Dennis, author of *The Sentimental Bloke*. Arden, the 'Singing Garden' he and his wife Biddy created, is ◷open daily 10am-5pm. The 1.5ha rhododendron gardens are a delight, and there are Tea Rooms where you can spend some time admiring them, and enjoying a light lunch. Across the road is Toolangi Pottery, where master potter David Williams produces and displays his stoneware and crystalline pottery. His work has been exhibited in the National Gallery of Victoria.

Wineries

The Yarra Valley has many wineries, and here they are listed, with the cellar door hours.
Yarra Burn Vineyard, Settlement Road, Yarra Junction, ◷5967 1428 -◷open daily 10am-6pm.
McWilliams Lillydale Vineyards, Davross Court, Seville, ◷5964 2016 - ◷open daily 11am-5pm.
Five Oaks Vineyard, Aitken Road, Seville, ◷5964 3704 - ◷open daily 10am-5pm.
Kelly Brook Winery, Fulford Road, Wonga Park, ◷9722 1304 - ◷open Wed-Sat 9am-6pm, Sun 11am-6pm, Mon 9am-6pm.
Bianchet Winery, Victoria Road, Lilydale, ◷9739 1779 -◷open Mon-Fri please phone prior to visit, Sat-Sun 10am-6pm.
Warramate Vineyard, Maddens Lane, Gruyere, ◷5964 9219 - ◷open daily10am-6pm.

Healesville Sanctuary

Yarra Valley

St Huberts Vineyard, St Huberts Road, Coldstream, ℂ9739 1118 -⏱Mon-Fri 9.30am-5pm, Sat 10.30am-5.30pm, Sun 11.30am-5.30pm.

Eyton On Yarra Winery & Restaurant, cnr Maroondah Highway & Hill Road, Coldstream, ℂ5962 2119 - ⏱daily 10am-5pm.

Fergusson's Winery & Restaurant, Wills Road, Yarra Glen, ℂ5965 2237 - ⏱ Mon-Fri 9am-5pm, Sat-Sun 11am-5pm.

De Bortoli Winery & Restaurant, Pinnacle Lane, Dixons Creek, ℂ5965 2271 - ⏱daily10am-5pm.

Shantell Vineyard, Melba Highway (60km post), Dixons Creek, ℂ5965 2155 - ⏱Thu-Mon 10.30am-5pm.

Broussard's Chum Creek Winery, Cunninghams Road, Healesville, ℂ5962 5551 - ⏱Sat-Sun 10am-6pm.

Long Gully Estate, Long Gully Road, Healesville, ℂ9510 798 - ⏱Mon-Fri please phone prior to visit, Sat-Sun noon-5pm.

Festivals

The Yarra Valley Expo, celebrating the regions wine, food and farmlife, is held in March.

Facilities

Lawn bowls, swimming, tennis, golf, fishing, greyhound racing, horseracing, harness racing and squash. There is a cinema on the highway.

Outlying Attractions

Marysville

Situated 36km (22 miles) north-east of Healesville, Marysville is high in the Great Dividing Range, 500m (1640 ft) above sea level. It has great forests, tree-fern gullies and is a cool and welcome retreat. In winter, nearby Lake Mountain offers one of the best cross-country ski areas outside Scandinavia.

There is an 18-hole golf course, and horse riding on mountain trails is available. Bushwalking is also a popular pastime.

Steavenson Falls, the tallest in Victoria, cascade 82m (269 ft) in three leaps and are flood-lit at night.

Accommodation is available in guesthouses, holiday lodges, cabins and motels, as well as a camping and caravan park beside the Steavenson River. For more information on Marysville, contact the Visitor Information Centre, 11 Murchison Street, ℂ(03) 5963 4567.

Eildon and Alexandra

These towns are the gateways to Lake Eildon and Fraser National Park. Both have facilities for fishing, bushwalking, camping, water skiing, swimming, sailing, cross country skiing, golf, tennis, squash and bowls, and accommodation is plentiful.

Alexandra is 69km (43 miles) north of Healesville, and Eildon is 26km (16 miles) east of Alexandra.

There are quite a few attractions - art and craft shops and galleries; fauna parks with native animals, deer and camels; The Timber Tramway & Museum at the old railway station, Alexandra, ℂ5772 2392; and the Visitor Centre at 45a Grant Street, Alexandra, ℂ(03) 5772 1100 will assist with further enquiries.

Warburton

this town is a mountain retreat in the heart of the Warburton Ranges. Popular as a conference venue, attractions include the beautfiul Donna Buang Rainforest Gallery and the jungle skywalk. There are also the stunning river walks, providing a unique opportunity to enjoy the Yarra River at its best. This small town boasts six bridges, so easy to choose the length of your walk. For more information contact the **Warburton Water Wheel and Visitor Centre** on ℂ(03) 5966 5996 or at: ✏ info@warburton-ranges.net.au

Bright & the Victorian Alps

Population - 1,800
Bright is situated on the Ovens River, in the foothills of the Victorian Alps. It is 310km (193 miles) from Melbourne, 700km (435 miles) from Sydney, 940km (584 miles from Adelaide, 74km (46 miles) from Wangaratta, and 116km (72 miles) from Albury.

Characteristics

Bright is truly a town for all seasons. In Summer, there is the river for safe swimming and fishing, and horseriding and bush walking are very popular. In Autumn, the European and Asian trees left by the pioneers become a blaze of gold, orange, red and yellow, and the town celebrates with the Autumn Festival. Winter brings snow to the mountains surrounding Bright, and the skiers arrive in their thousands for the slopes in the three close alpine resorts. And in Spring, the elms, poplars, wattles, fruit trees, etc, create the brightest Bright of all.

How to Get There

By Bus
Greyhound Pioneer travel to Albury-Wodonga from Sydney and Melbourne, and connect with a local bus service to Bright.

By Rail
Regular train services run from Melbourne and Sydney to Wangaratta, and then V-line buses to Bright.

By Road
From Melbourne, either via the Hume Highway to Wangaratta and then the Ovens Highway, or via the Princes Highway to Bairnsdale and then the Omeo Highway.

From Sydney, via the Hume Highway to Albury, then the Kiewa Valley Highway.

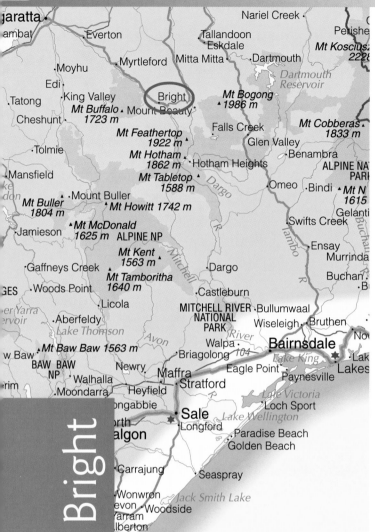

Tourist Information

The Bright Tourist Information Centre is at 119 Gavan Street, ✆(03) 5755 2275 or ✆1800 500 117, ✉email bright@dragnet.com.au

Two websites to visit are 👁www. brightdistrict.com.au (for limited local information) and 👁www. alpinelink.com.au

Accommodation

Bright's main industry is tourism, so there is no shortage of accommodation. Here we have a selection, with prices for a double room per night, which should be used as a guide only. The telephone area code is 03.

Barrass's John Bright Motor Inn, 10 Wood Street, ✆5755 1400. 20 units, pool, spa, bbq - ✪$85-145.

High Country Inn, 13 Gavan Street, ✆5755 1244. 32 units, licensed restaurant, swimming pool, spa, sauna, bbq - ✪$89-112.

Acacia Motor Lodge, 85 Gavan Street, ✆5755 1441. 12 units, pool, bbq - ✪$77-125.

Bright Avenue Motor Inn, 87 Delany Avenue, ✆5755 1911. 13 units, bbq - ✪$77-130.

Ovens Valley Motor Inn, cnr Great Alpine Rd & Ashwood Avenue, ✆5755 2022. 24 units, restaurant, pool, spa, sauna, bbq - ✪$75-95.

Bright Motor Inn, 1 Delany Avenue, ✆5750 1433. 26 units, restaurant, bbq - ✪$60-75.

Riverbank Park Motel, 69 Gavan Street, ✆5755 1255. 24 units, restaurant, pool - ✪$88-100.

Bright Colonial Inn Motel, 54 Gavan Street, ✆5755 1197. 18 rooms (private facilities), restaurant, bbq - ✪$77-88.

Caravan Parks

Alpine Cabins & Caravan Park, 1 Mountbatten Avenue, ✆5755 1064. (No pets allowed) - powered sites ✪$20-25 for two, cabins $57-115 for two.

Bright Caravan Park, Cherry Avenue, ✆5755 1141. (No dogs allowed Christmas, January and Easter) - powered sites ✪$17-25 for two, park cabins (en-suite) $50-100 for two, park cabins (standard) $40 -56 for two.

Bright Riverside Holiday Park, 4 Toorak Avenue, ✆5755 1118. (No pets) - powered sites ✪$17-26 for two, cabins $25-33 for two.

Green Hills Caravan Park, Great Alpine Rd, ✆5750 1218. (Pets allowed on leash) - powered sites ✪$16-22 for two, on-site vans $29-41 for two.

Eating Out

Many of the hotels and motels have dining rooms, and there are the usual amount of takeaway outlets for a holiday town. Here are some you might like to try:

Lawler's Hut, 100 Gavan St, Bright, ⓒ1800 813 992 - licensed, high quality local produce - a la carte - open for breakfast and dinner.

Poplars, 8 Star Road, Bright, ⓒ5755 1655 - BYO and licensed, a la carte and seafood - open daily from 6.30pm.

The Cosy Kangaroo, Gavan Street, ⓒ5750 1838 - good value family restaurant.

Ned's Rstaurant & Bar, 13-17 Gavan Street, ⓒ5755 1244 - licensed, country-style dining - open Tue-Sat for dinner.

Golden Bright Chinese Restaurant, 108 Gavan Street, ⓒ5750 1155.

Simone's Restaurant, cnr Ovens Highway & Ashwood Avenue, ⓒ5755 2022.

Tin Dog Cafe & Pizzeria, 94 Gavan Street, ⓒ5755 1526.

Points of Interest

The pretty village of Bright sparkles against its backdrop of dark green-clad hills, and is one of Australia's longest established holiday destinations, having welcomed visitors for more than a century. Bright's first guide book was published in 1887, and included maps of walking tracks and bridle paths, specially marked and graded according to degree of difficulty. These are still popular today, and current maps are available at the Tourist Information centre. Some of the most popular walks are to the Clearspot, Huggins and Mt Porepunkah lookouts, which offer a panoramic view of the village.

The **Historical Museum of Bright** has been established in the town's disused railway station. It is ⓒopen 2-4pm Tue, Thu & Sun during school holidays and festivals, and 2-4pm Sun from September to May.

The **Bright Art Gallery & Cultural Centre**, 28 Mountbatten Avenue, ⓒ5750 1660, has a comprehensive art collection and a gem and rare mineral collection, as well as the largest cuckoo clock in Australia. It is ⓒopen Mon-Sat 1-5pm, Sun 9am-5.30pm, and daily during school holidays.

Gallery 90, 90 Gavan Street, ⓒ5755 1385, has original paintings, pottery, leather, handpainted clothing, jewellery, handpainted porcelain, traditional cottage crafts, and much more. The gallery is housed in a restored local granite

and bluestone cottage that dates back to 1881, and is ⓒopen Mon-Sat 9.30am-5.30pm, Sun 11am-5.30pm. During the Autumn Festival the hours are extended to 9am-5.30pm daily.

Walks around Bright are marked by sign posts and yellow track markers fixed to trees and posts. Maps and guides are available from the newsagent and the Tourist Information Centre for walks further afield, and if venturing up in the hills you should remember to take some warm clothing, as it will be colder there than down in the valley. The climb to **Mt Buffalo** commences at the Park entrance and climbs through 11km (7 miles) of varied scenery, to arrive at the oval

Bright

Paragliding in Bright

Bright

below the *Mt Buffalo Chalet*.

For the less energetic, there is a wide variety of **tours**, both half and full day, to various attractions around Bright and the high country. For further information and bookings, contact the Tourist Information Centre. If you are in Bright in the winter, enquire about ski packages and snow trips.

Festivals

The Bright Autumn Festival is held during the last week of April and the first week of May each year, and one of the main features is Gala Day with street processions and stalls. The entrants for Miss Autumn Festival are received at the Presentation Ball and the judging and crowning takes place.

Among the many events that are part of the Festival are: the opening of the Autumn Art Exhibition; conducted tours of tobacco farms; gold panning exhibitions; historic tours of Wandiligong and surrounding districts; tours of the forests by the Forest Commission; a Family Picnic; an Old Time Music Hall; and wine and cheese tastings.

The Springtime in Bright Festival is held during October and November, and co-ordinates a whole range of events and activities.

Outlying Attractions

Porepunkah
The small town of Porepunkah is 6km (4 miles) from Bright, at the junction of the Buckland and Ovens Rivers, and the turnoff to Mount Buffalo National Park. Originally named Port Punka, the area was part of a cattle station which reached from Eurobin to Bright. During the gold mining era, the township site was known as The Ovens Crossing. It is a quiet, peaceful spot, and has a hotel, post office,

petrol station, general store, several riverside caravan parks, and a growing number of flats and motels. The two rivers provide excellent fishing for trout.

The Snow Country

The major ski centres are Falls Creek, Mt Buffalo and Mt Hotham. The website ☞www.ski.com.au gives the latest information about the weather and skiing conditions at all the Victorian ski resorts. Ski packages and snow trips to the three resorts can be arranged thorugh various outlets, and the Tourist Centre can provide you with a list of operators and prices.

Mount Buffalo

The mountain is 32km (20 miles) from Bright, and 320km (199 miles) from Melbourne. Accommodation on the slopes is available at Mount Buffalo Chalet and Lodge, and inclusive packages are offered.

Operating only 3 poma lifts and 2 chairlifts, Mt Buffalo is a small, sheltered ski field that focuses on laid-back family enjoyment. It is comprised mainly of gentle downhill slopes. Serious skiiers looking for a challenge should head elsewhere, although cross-country ski trails are available here in Mt Buffalo National Park.

Lift ticket prices are $39 adult, $25 child for one day; $180 adult, $120 child for 5 days; and $199 for a season pass.

Mount Buffalo Chalet, ☏(03) 5755 1500, ☞www.mtbuffalo chalet.com.au. You can choose from the guesthouses, which have shared facilties, or the View and Tower rooms, which are private. Prices include dinner, breakfast, activities, guided walks, shuttle transfers daily, entry into the National Park, and use of all Chalet facilities. They should be used as a guide only.

Guesthouse - 2 nights $260 adult, $140 child; 5 nights (including lunch) $670 adult, $350 child.

View Room - 2 nights $370 adult, $160 child; 5 nights $865 (including lunch) adult, $395 child.

Tower Room - 2 nights $395 adult, $160 child; 5 nights (including lunch) $920 adult, $395 child.

The nearby Mount Buffalo Lodge offers motel and lodge-style accommodation with breakfast, use of facilities and National Park entry included, and backpacker rooms with meals not included.

Motel - 2 nights $130 adult, $55 child; 3 nights $180 adult, $85 child.

Lodge - 2 nights $105 adult, $55 child; 3 nights $150 adult, $85 child.

Backpackers - 2 nights $40 adult, $35 child; 3 nights $65 adult, $50 child.

Ski hire is available and ski lessons can be booked.

Dingo Dell

Ski runs are 6km (4 miles) south of the Chalet, and are ideal for beginners and family groups. There are two poma lifts and a portable beginners' lift.

Amenities and services include the large car park within easy walking distance of the slopes; ski instruction; Keown Lodge, a visitor centre which is used as a day lodge and provides takeaway and eat-in meals, changing rooms, toilets and first aid facilities.

Cresta Valley

Ski runs are 4km (2 miles) south of Dingo Dell, and are around the Mt Buffalo Lodge & Alpine Resort, ☏5755 1988, at about 1525m (5003 ft) above sea level. There are eight runs served by 5 lifts catering for beginner, intermediate and advanced skiers. The degree of difficulty of a slope can be identified by the coloured markers at the runs. Easiest runs are marked by green circles and are served by the Gully Poma and Novice Poma. More difficult runs are marked with blue squares and suit intermediate skiers. The Valley and Cresta Chairlift runs are in this category. The most difficult runs are marked by black diamonds and are reached by riding the Cresta Poma.

Bright

Falls Creek

Victorian Alps

The Cresta Day Visitor Centre houses the resort management office, ski school, ticket office, National Park information area, medical centre and a cafe offering takeaway.

Cross Country Trails are graded Beginner and Intermediate, with access to Cresta Valley graded Intermediate to Advanced. Lift Tickets: Ticket boxes have single ride, half-day and full day; Cresta Office has a season pass (photo required); and The Chalet and Tatra Inn have 1-day, 2-day, 3-day, 5-day and 7-day packages.

Falls Creek
👁www.fallscreek.com.au
Falls Creek is 62km (39 miles) from Bright, 32km (20 miles) from the township of Mount Beauty, and 356km (221 miles) from Melbourne. There are many guest houses to choose from, and several offer ski packages.

Falls Creek has snowmaking machines, and the system covers 10ha (25 acres). It is installed on Towers Duplex, Panorama, Playground, Tom Thomb and at the top of Eagle, Halley's Comet and Scott Chairlifts.

Following is a brief description of the ski runs

Novice
Nursery Pomas/Dogpatch Pomas - in the bowl area, near the Ski School. Ideal for beginners.

Saddle Linklift - an easy T-Bar for skiers of all standards. Also gives access to the Ruined Castle area.

Headwater Poma, Playground Pomas, Tom Thumb - gentle and have easy access via the Eagle Chair and Halley's Comet Quad Chair, returning via the Broadway Hometrail and the Wombat's Ramble Home-trail.

Halley's Comet Quad Chairlift - a fast access lift from the carpark to the slopes of Sun Valley. Novice skiers return via the Wombat's Ramble Hometrail and intermediates return via the Last Hoot Hometrail. At the top of Halley's Comet is the Cloud Nine Restaurant with bar, dining and restroom facilities.

Intermediate
Gully Triple Chairlift - an access lift from the carpark to the bowl. Gully slopes are not suitable for novices.

Village T-Bar - forming part of the sheltered bowl, these runs are ideal for easy intermediate skiing.

Panorama Poma, Towers Duplex T-Bar, Lakeside Poma, Scott Quad

Chairlift, Ruined Castle Poma - these five lifts offer a variety of intermediate skiing. The valley holds a good cover of dry snow on interesting gullies and lightly wooded trails.

Eagle Triple Chairlift - a fast access lift from the bowl to the slopes of Sun Valley. Return via the Broadway Hometrail.

Advanced
Big Dipper Duplex T-Bar - a good length run for intermediate skiers. However, on the right-hand side is a large cornice with deep soft snow.

Summit T-Bar - known traditionally as the advanced skier's paradise, the finest bumps run in Australia.

International Poma - a fast lift providing challenging skiing for advanced skiers. Also provides access to the Bowl, the Summit, and the slopes of Sun Valley.

Lift Tickets
A full range of lift tickets is available early in the morning at Bogong Ski Centre, Kiewa Valley Highway, Mt Beauty, and at JD's Mountain Sports, cnr Burke & Anderson Streets, Bright. They can also be purchased in the Sun Valley area. Passport type photographs are required for Season and 4, 5, 6 and 7 day lift,

and lift and lesson packages. Instant photos can be taken at Cumings, The Hub, Gebi's, Snowland and The Creek Photo Service. 4, 5, 6 and 7 days lift, and lift and lesson tickets can be purchased after 4pm on day prior to the first day of use.

Approximate prices are: Half day - $56 adult, $29 child; 1 day - $75 adult, $39 child; 2 day - $144 adult, $74 child; 3 day - $212 adult, $108 child; 4 day - $273 adult, $140 child; 5 day - $328 adult, $171 child; 6 day - $383 adult, $199 child; 7 day - $420 adult, $218 child.

Season tickets cost between $400 and $900, depending on the time of purchase - the earlier the better.

A one day lift & lesson package costs $105 adult, $70 child. Ski hire is available.

Accommodation
Below is a selection of what is available in the heart of Falls Creek. All have outstanding views of the surrounding mountains.

Alpha Lodge, ✆5758 3488, from $23 for shared rooms and $41 for a single room, per person.

Falls Creek Country Club, ✆5758 3391, from $135 for a double room.

Alpine View & Cumings Apartments, ✆5758 3461, from $420 for a 4-room apartment.

Attunga Alpine Lodge & Apartments, ✆5758 3255, from $100 for a double room, including breakfast.

Alpine Woodsmoke, ✆5754 1138, www.woodsmoke.com.au, apartments from $200 per night.

Mount Hotham
👁www.mthotham.com.au

Mount Hotham is 55km (34 miles) from Bright, and 354km (220 miles) from Melbourne. It is Australia's highest alpine village at 1750m (5741 ft), and all accommodation is only minutes from the ski runs. The runs are classified as 27% beginner, 36% interme-

Victorian Alps

Mount Hotham

diate and 37% advanced.

More information can be obtained from the Mount Hotham Alpine Resort Management Board, Great Alpine Road, Mount Hotham, ℂ(03) 5759 3550, send emails to ✎ mhar@mthotham.com.au

There are over 40 marked and groomed runs on the slopes, and the ski school, ticket sales, ski shops and ski hire are all in easy walking distance from the car parks, and one short step from the slopes.

Above the Village
Summit - a high altitude slope of south-easterly aspect, and a reliable beginners' area. Served by the Summit quad chairlift, and on the summit is the Doppelmayr T-Bar.

Big D - at the southern end of Mt Hotham village, with reliable snow and gentle beginners' slopes.

Below the Village
Sun Run - opposite the Summit, the Sun Run is for skiers progressing to intermediate. Served by a T-Bar lift.

Basin - a sheltered bowl opposite the main day car-park offering skiing for beginners and intermediates. Served by a Doppelmayr platter lift.

Playground - several trails for intermediate and advanced skiers down to Swindlers Creek.

Heavenly Valley
The Heavenly Valley quad chairlift provides access to vast areas of skiing terrain for confident intermediates and advanced skiers.

Blue Ribbon - served by a Doppelmayr triple chairlift, offers sustained and sheltered fall line skiing for intermediate and advanced skiers.

Mt Hotham Village offers a range of shops and services including ski hire, ski shop, licensed restaurants (Italian, international and modern Australian), pizzeria, a supermarket, bistro, post office, nightclub and information desk.

Lift Tickets
Lift passes are available from the Mount Hotham Skiing Company, ℂ5759 4444, which has an office on the mountain.

The following are prices for lifts only. Half day - $56 adult, $29 child; 1 day - $75 adult, $39 child; 2 day - $144 adult, $74 child; 3 day - $212 adult, $108 child; 5 day - $328 adult, $171 child; 7 day - $420 adult, $218 child; Season - from $870 adult, $440 child.

Myrtleford
Situated 29km (18 miles) north-west of Bright on the Ovens Highway, Myrtleford is at the foot of Mount Buffalo. The district's main industries are timber, hops, tobacco and cattle.

The town has 3 hotels, 2 motels, a caravan park, 2 camping reserves, bunkhouse and lodge accommodation. There are facilities for swimming, tennis, golf, bowls, bocce, croquet, fishing (trout and redfin), horse riding, hang gliding, bush-walking, and of course, skiing.

Shepparton

Population 32,000
Shepparton is located in the Lower Goulburn Valley in the northern 'centre' of Victoria, 178km (111 miles) north of Melbourne.

Climate

Average temperatures: January max 30C (86F) - min 14C (57F); July max 13C (55F) - min 4C(39F). Average annual rainfall: 502mm (20 ins). Shepparton averages more than 7 hours of sunlight per day.

Characteristics

Shepparton was declared The Solar City by the Solar Council in 1986, due to the large amount of sunshine it averages, and the city has a solar heated swimming pool (in summer), some solar powered street lighting in areas, a solar powered telephone outside the Tourist Information Centre, and some solar powered parking meters. It is the major city of the Goulburn Valley, one of the food bowls of the nation. The area produces enormous quantities of fruit, vegetables and dairy products, as well as cereal crops, grapes, wine, beef, wool and lamb.

How to Get There

By Rail

V/Line Trains have services Mon-Fri from Spencer Street Station in Melbourne, leaving at 9.10am and 6.15pm. On Saturday the trains leave at 9.10am and 6.10pm, and on Sunday at 9.50am and 6.05pm.

By Bus

Greyhound Pioneer stop at Shepparton on their Melbourne/Brisbane service. V/Line coaches have services from Melbourne daily except Saturday.

How to Get There - Continued

By Road

From Melbourne, via the Hume Highway to north of Shepparton, then the Goulburn Valley Highway.

From Sydney, via the Hume Highway to Benalla, then the Midland Highway.

Eating Out

Cellar 47 Restaurant, 166 -170 High Street, ℂ5831 1882, is open for lunch Tues-Fri noon-2pm, dinner Tues-Sat from 6pm.

Shepparton Family Restaurant, City Walk, ℂ5821 3737, specialise in Chinese and Australian smorgasbord - open for lunch Mon-Sat 11.30am-2.30pm, dinner every day 5.30-9.30pm.

Parklake Motor Inn Cafe Bar Restaurant, at the Parklake Motor Inn, 481 Wyndham Street, ℂ5821 5822, is open for dinner nightly from 6pm, and has a dinner dance on Saturdays.

La Porchetta, 264 Maude Street, ℂ5821 0800 - Italian and pizza.

Casablanca Pizza Restaurant, 125 High Street, ℂ5821 1115 - takeaway available.

New China Restaurant, 55 Fryers Street, ℂ5831 1166.

Calzoneys Restaurant, 30 North Street, ℂ5831 3578.

Aloi Thai Restaurant, 630a Wyndham Street, ℂ5831 6613.

Riviera Pizza Restaurant, 117a Wyndham Street , ℂ5821 4402.

Pizza Hut is at 525 Wyndham Street, ℂ5822 2111, and *KFC* has two outlets in Wyndham Street at nos 620 and 465.

Accommodation

There is a wide range to choose from, and here is a selection with prices for a double room per night, which should be used as a guide only. The telephone area code is 03.

Parklake Motor Inn, 481 Wyndham Street, ℂ5821 5822. 70 units, licensed restaurant, swimming pool, spa, sauna - ✪$116-176.

Pines Country Club Motor Inn, 103 Numurkah Road, ℂ5831 2044. 20 units, licensed restaurant (closed Sunday), pool - ✪$110-130.

Paradise Lakes Motel Resort, 7685 Goulburn Valley Highway, Shep-parton South, ℂ5823 1888. 26 units(private facilities), swimming pool, spa, bbq - ✪$80-115.

Tirana Motor Inn, 33 Wyndham Street(Goulburn Valley Hwy), ℂ5831 1766. 24 units, swimming pool, bbq - ✪$80-90.

The Bel-Air Motor Inn, 630 Wyndham Street (Goulburn Valley Hwy), ℂ5821 4833. 30 units, licensed restaurant (closed Monday), swimming pool, spa, sauna - ✪$65-80.

Country Home Motor Inn, 11 *Wyndham Street*, ℂ5821 7711. 15 units, pool, bbq - ✪$65-80.

Overlander Hotel/Motel, 97 Benalla Road (Midland Hwy), ℂ5821 5622. 30 units, licensed restaurant, pool - ✪$65-70.

Apex Motel, Goulburn Valley Highway, ℂ5821 4472. 16 units, pool, bbq - ✪$45-50.

Victoria Hotel Shepparton, cnr Wyndham & Fryers Streets, ℂ5821 9955. 37 rooms, licensed restaurant - ✪$40-65.

Caravan Parks

Pine Lodge Caravan Park, cnr Midland Highway & Orrvale Road, ℂ5829 2396. (No pets) - powered sites ✪$19-22 for two, no site vans.

Shepparton Riverview Caravan Park, Melbourne Road (Goulburn Valley Hwy), ℂ5823 1561. (Dogs allowed at manager's discretion) - powered sites ✪$16 for two, no on-site vans.

Strayleaves Caravan Park, cnr Mitchell Street & Old Dookie Road, ℂ5821 1232. (No dogs allowed) - powered sites ✪$16 for two, on-site vans $29 for two.

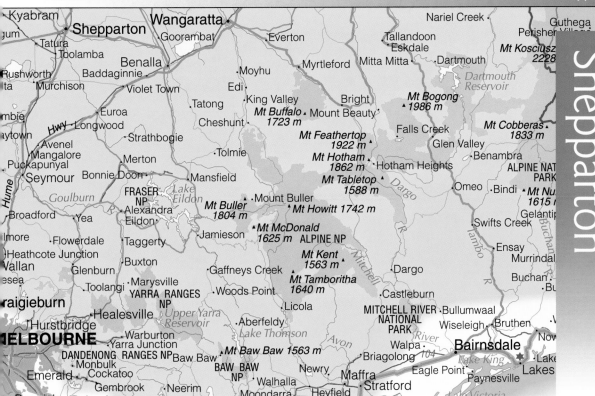

Visitor Information

The Tourist Information Centre, Victoria Park Lake, 534 Wyndham Street, ℰ(03) 5831 4400 or ℰ1800 808 839, is ☉open 10am-3pm daily. Further information is available online at ☀www.shepparton.vic. gov.au and you can email ✉visitor@shepparton.vic.gov.au

Points of Interest

Victoria Park Lake, near where the Tourist Information Centre is found, has picnic, barbecue, water skiing, windsurfing and cycling facilities. It is the leisure centre of the city.

The **Eastbank Centre** in Welsford Street, which houses the town hall, art gallery, theatre and municipal offices, is one of the most outstanding in any rural city in Australia. It was designed by architecture students from the University of Melbourne.

The **Shepparton Art Gallery**, in the Eastbank, has an extensive collection of ceramic works by well known artists, and around 150 paintings including pieces by McCubbin. It is ☉open 10am-4pm seven days, and admission is free, ℰ5832 9861.

The **Historical Museum**, cnr Welsford & High Streets, is ☉open on irregular Sundays 1-4pm (ℰ5831 4400), and has exhibits of local memorabilia from Aboriginal and European heritage to current events.

The **Telecommunications Tower** in Fraser Street, West Walk of the Maude Street Mall, has an observation platform which allows 360 degree views of the district. At the base of the tower is a Human Sundial, which accurately tells the time when you stand on the point corresponding to the day's date.

Maude Street Mall is in the heart of the city and is a shopping centre with many features including entertainment areas, loads of trees and flower beds, and plenty of parking.

Shepparton

Shepparton Preserving Company (SPC), Andrew Fairley Avenue, has a sales outlet ◷open Mon-Fri, and factory tours during the canning season, January-April.

Driver Education Centre of Australia (DECA), Wanganui Road, ◷5821 1099, has courses for people of all ages, and tours of the complex are ◷available Mon-Fri 8am-5pm.

In the **Shepparton Sports Stadium**, near McEwan Reserve, is a Maze which will keep all the family involved for a while.

Radio Australia in Verney Road, Lemnos, is home of the international broadcasting station. Tours by appointment, ◷5829 9202.

The **Dookie College of Agriculture and Horticulture**, is midway between Shepparton and Benalla. The buildings are situated at the foot of Mt Major, fringing the Goulburn Valley, and have excellent accommodation, conference and seminar facilities, ◷5833 9200.

Festivals

The Sun City Festival is held over seven days in March/April, and the Shepparton Show is in October.

Kialla West Strawberry Festival is held in November.

Facilities

Sporting facilities include horse-racing, trotting, greyhound racing, tennis, squash, lawn bowls, golf, and water sports. There is a cinema, cnr Maude & Stuart Streets, and a drive-in theatre in Melbourne Road, South Shepparton.

Outlying Attractions

Numurkah

Situated 35km (22 miles) north of Shepparton on the Goulburn Valley Highway, Numurkah has a population of around 3000, and is on Broken Creek. The town is surrounded by mostly irrigated farmland, with a wide range of crops. There is also wool and beef production, and a large dairying industry.

The town is about the same distance from the Murray River, and its attractions include the Barmah Forest, Monichino Wines (◷5864 6452), Brookfield Historic Farm (◷5862 2353), and of course, the Murray River beaches.

The Numurkah Visitor Information Centre is at 25 Quinn Street, ◷(03) 5862 3458.

Tocumwal

This is the first New South Wales town on the Newell Highway, and is situated on the banks of the Murray River. It offers a blend of old with new, from Federation era buildings with stained glassed windows to modern licensed clubs, business and accommodation developments.

The town has a population of around 1400, but this is regularly swelled with visitors stopping off on their north or south journeys. There is a golf club and a bowling club with first class facilities, restaurants, and being in New South Wales - poker machines. The main street of the town and the river are divided by parklands with camping sites, water skiing, swimming, boating, sailing and fishing facilities, and houseboat cruises departure points. About 2km from town there is a wartime aerodrome where Sportavia Soaring (Gliding) Centre offers year-round gliding, ◷5874 2063.

The Visitor Information Centre is in Foreshore Park, ◷(03) 5874 2131.

Mount Buller

◉www.mtbuller.com.au

The ski village is 47km (29 miles) from Mansfield, and is situated at 1600m (5249 ft), with the highest lifted point at 1788m (5866 ft). There are 5 Poma, 8 T-bar, 4 Triple chair and 7 Quad chair lifts, with

a capacity of 38,500 people an hour.

The downhill skiable area is 162ha (400 acres), and is graded 24% Beginner, 34% Intermediate and 42% Advanced, with the longest run 2500m (2734 yds).

The Cross-Country areas are Village Loop (Beginner) and Corn Hill (Beginner), with total trails of 10.9km (7 miles).

Lift Tickets: Day - adult $70, child (under 16) $40; Half day - adult $60, child $30; Five day - adult $300, child $200; Seven day - adult $420, child $280; Season - adult $1000, child $560.

Accommodation is available in the village area at **Pension Grimus**, ©5777 6396 - $390-440 for a double room; and **Arlberg Hotel**, ©1800 032 380 - DBB one person $140 per night twin share. Contact Mt Buller Resort Management for other accommodation options, call ©(03) 5777 6077 or send an email to ✉ info@mtbuller.com.au

Mansfield

Situated 63km (39 miles) south of Benalla, at the terminus of both the Maroondah and Midland Highways, Mansfield is the gateway to the Mount Buller alpine resort.

The town is also close to the north arm of Lake Eildon, and to Lake Nillahcootie, so in summer is a popular spot for fishing, sailing, water skiing and white water canoeing. In winter the skiers move into town. This area was the setting for the classic *The Man From Snowy River* movies, and that beautiful scenery was not trick photography, as visitors soon discover.

Call in at the Mansfield Visitor Information Centre at the Railway Station on the Maroondah Highway, ©(03) 5775 1464.

Benalla

Benalla is 61km (38 miles) south-east of Shepparton, at the junction of the Hume and Midland Highways. The Visitor Information Centre is at 14 Mair Street, ©(03) 5762 1749.

Benalla was the base of operations in the

Camel Trekking in the High Country near Mansfield

1870s for the Kelly Gang, and many mementoes of the Gang can be found in the Kelly Museum in Bridge Street. Enquire at the Visitor Centre about opening times.

Benalla is also famous for its roses, and from late October until early April the Benalla Gardens provide the finest display of that bloom in the State. The Rose Festival is held each November.

The Benalla Art Gallery, in the Benalla Gardens, ©5762 3833, has an impressive collection of Australian art, including several paintings from the Heidelberg School by Roberts, Streeton and McCubbin.

Violet Town

Situated 13km (8 miles) west of Benalla, Violet Town is on Honeysuckle Creek and at the foothills of the Strathbogie Ranges. It is the oldest surveyed inland town in Victoria, having been surveyed in 1838, but there was no

Shepparton

permanent settlement until 1846. There is a caravan park, hotels, a swimming pool, and many sporting facilities.
Head out to the Stonecrop Fine Art Gallery on Harry's Creek Road, ℂ5798 1444, ⏱between 11am and 5pm any day, and enjoy their dispays and garden surrounds.

Euroa

Euroa is 45km (28 miles) west of Benalla. The Euroa district is steeped in history from the time of early settlement in the 1800s, prospering from people heading for the goldfields. The first flock of Saxon Merino sheep in the State was driven overland from New South Wales to Euroa, and since that time wool has played the major part in the development of Euroa.

Seven Creeks winds through the town with parkland on both banks, and the "Seven Creeks Run" has been established, a project depicting the history of the wool industry. International shearing competitions are conducted in Euroa, and Wool Week has become an event known throughout Australia.

The surrounding district, which includes Forlonge Memorial and Strathbogie Ranges, appeals to the trout fisherman and the bushwalker.

Seymour

Situated at the northern foothills of the Great Dividing Range on the Goulburn River, Seymour is 84km (52 miles) south of Shepparton, and only one hour's drive from Melbourne. The Panyule Fauna Park & Tourist Information Centre, on the corner of Seymour-Tooboorac and Pyalong Roads, can be contacted on ℂ(03) 5799 0043.

A short distance to the north of the town is Mangalore Airport, originally built as an alternate airport for Melbourne. It is now the headquarters of the Australian Sport Aviation Council, and the Mangalore Air Spectacular

Show is held annually over the Easter weekend.

Attractions in the area include:

Trawool Valley has been classified by the National Trust for its scenic beauty. There is an international standard resort, and tea rooms and a gallery. The century-old former Trawool Chool is an art gallery, ℂ5792 3118. Riddy's Trawool Valley Tours, ℂ5792 1654, is one way to see the area in full.

Avenel is a small township on Hughes Creek, some 20km (12 miles) from Seymour. It has a number of historical buildings, four of which have been classified by the National Trust, and the grave of Ned Kelly's father. Look out for the old Harvest 'Home Hotel, built in the 1860s and now a restaurant, ℂ5796 2339.

Puckapunyal Army Camp is 13km (8 miles) west of Seymour, off the Hume Freeway. The camp has the Royal Australian Armoured Corps Tank Museum, which may be viewed 10am-4pm daily, ℂ5793 7285.

Nagambie

The gateway to the Goulburn Valley, Nagambie is 28km (17 miles) north of Seymour. The township was founded in the mid-19th century and has a number of important historical buildings, seven of which are classified by the National Trust. The eastern shore of Lake Nagambie abuts the main street, with grassy picnic areas on its banks. Buckley Park, at the southern entrance of the town has a shady picnic area, boat launching ramp, and swimming area.

Lake Nagambie was created by the construction of the Goulburn Weir, which was built with manual labour in 1890. The River and Lake combine to offer over 40km (25 miles) of waterways for boating, and there are many picnic areas. The Nagambie Lakes Visitor Information Centre is at 145 High Street, ℂ(03) 5794 2647 or ℂ1800 444 647, and they have information on the many wineries in the area.

Bendigo

Population 40,340

Bendigo is almost in the centre of Victoria, at the junction of the Calder, McIvor, Northern and Loddon Valley Highways. It is 151km (94 miles) from Melbourne, 661km (411 miles) from Adelaide, 892km (554 miles) from Sydney and 653km (406 miles) from Canberra.

Climate

Average temperatures: January max 29C (84F) - min 14C (57F); July max 12C (54F) - min 3C (37F). Average annual rainfall: 550mm (22 in).

Characteristics

Bendigo was once one of the richest gold mining towns in Australia. It is proud of its mining history and has preserved relics of the period for present and future generations. The most tangible of these is a complete mine in working condition, in the town - the Central Deborah Mine.

How to Get There

By Bus

Greyhound Pioneer stop at Bendigo on their Melbourne/Mildura routes. A mini-bus service operates between Ballarat and Bendigo.

By Rail

A regular daily service operates between Melbourne and Bendigo, and the journey takes two hours. Bendigo is also linked by rail to Echuca, Cohuna, Swan Hill and Charlton.

By Road

From Melbourne by the Calder Highway is a two hour trip. From Albury/Wodonga, take the Hume Highway, then the Midland Highway for the 279km (173 miles) trip to Bendigo.

Bendigo

Accommodation

There are 24 motels, 7 hotels, 10 caravan parks and a youth hostel. Here is a selection, with prices for a double room per night, which should be used as a guide only. The telephone area code is 03.

All Seasons International Motor Inn, 171 McIvor Highway, 5443 8166. 49 units, licensed restaurant, pool, spa - $125-180.

Bendigo Colonial Motor Inn, 483 High Street, 5447 0122. 30 units, restaurant (closed Sunday), indoor pool, spa, sauna $120-180.

Central Deborah Motor Inn, 177 High St (Calder Hwy), 5443 7488. 26 units, licensed restaurant (closed Sunday), spa - $95-115.

Lakeview Motor Inn, 286 Napier Street, 5442 3099. 33 units, licensed restaurant (closed Sunday), pool, spa, bbq - $95-110.

Bendigo Motor Inn, 232 High Street, Kangaroo Flat, 5447 8555. 32 units, licensed restaurant (closed Sunday), swimming pool, spa, sauna, playground, bbq - $75-90.

Shamrock Hotel Bendigo, cnr Pall Mall & Williamson Street, 5443 0333. 30 rooms, licensed restaurant - $70-145.

The Elm Motel, 454 High St, 5447 7522. 15 rooms (private facilities) - $55-70.

Calder Motel, 296 High Street (Calder Hwy), Kangaroo Flat, 5447 7411. 12 units, swimming pool, bbq - $50-65.

Caravan Parks

Ascot Lodge, 15 Heinz Street, White Hills, 5448 4421. (No pets) - powered sites $20-22 for two, cabins (en-suite) $60-90 for two, cabins (standard) $45-55 for two.

Robinley Caravan Park, Calder Hwy, Maiden Gully, 5449 6265. (No pets) - powered sites $15-20 for two, on-site vans $35-40.

Central City Caravan Park, 362 High Street (Calder Hwy), Golden Square, 5443 6937. (Dogs allowed on leash) - powered sites $17 for two, on-site vans $35 for two.

Eating Out

There's a good range of restaurants and cafes in Bendigo, offering various types of cuisine. Pub lunches are widely available and usually represent good value. They range from the humble ploughman's lunch to hearty steak and vegies. Good restaurants include:

Bazzani, Howard Place, 5441 3777 - licensed - open 7 days.

Whirrakee Restaurant, 17 View Point, 5441 5557 - overlooks Alexandra Fountain - licensed - modern Australian cuisine.

Jo Joes, 4 High Street, 5441 4471 - international cuisine - changing menu - open 7 days for lunch and dinner.

The Boardwalk Restaurant & Cafe, Nolan Street, 5443 9833 - lakeside dining, open for breakfast lunch and dinner 7am-7pm daily - licensed.

Cafe Tram, 76 Violet Street, 5443 8255 - licensed - bookings essential - open for dinner Fri & Sat, lunch on Sun.

Malayan Orchid Restaurant, 157 View Street, 5442 4411 - Thai, Cantonese and Malaysian curries - open Mon-Fri 12-2pm, dinner seven days.

Fortunes Restaurant, 171 McIvor Road, 5443 8166 - open 7 days - a la carte - lunch and dinner - licensed.

There is also a *Pizza Hut* on the corner of High & Violet Streets, 5443 2122, and *McDonald's* is at 63 High Street.

Tourist Information

The Bendigo Visitor Information & Interpretive Centre is located inhe Historic Post Office, 51-67 Pall Mall, (03) 5444 4445 or 1800 813 153. It is open seven days a week 9am-5pm. You can send emails to the addres tourism@bendigo.vic.gov.au or visit the website www.bendigo tourism.com Another website, for the wider region, is www. goldfields.org.au, but it is less detailed.

Points of Interest

The heart of Bendigo is well worth exploring on foot, with much to see and admire in the busy shopping area and nearby parks. The Vintage Talking Trams will take you to many other places of interest. A Bendigo Heritage Walk leaflet is available from the Information Centre.

Bendigo has been described as, architecturally, the most interesting and in-tegrated provincial city in Australia. Solidly built with the wealth that gold gave it, the city has some of the best preserved Victorian-era buildings and street-scapes to be found anywhere.

Alexandra Fountain is situated at the head of Bendigo's Pall Mall, Charing Cross. The fountain was a gift from George Lansell 'the quartz king'. Designed by W.C. Vahland, erected in 1881 and made from 20 tonnes of granite, it features seahorses and nymphs.

Central Deborah Gold Mine, 76 Violet Street, ℗5443 8322. The last deep-reef goldmine in Bendigo - sunk in 1909, closed in 1954 - has been restored and is open for inspection. It is 411m (135 ft) deep with 17 levels. The tourist level at 61m (200 ft) includes a 350m (383 yds) circuit which illustrates the various geological features of the Bendigo region, and the machinery used in the gold retrieval process. Above ground there are many exhibits to be inspected. The mine is open - daily 9.30am-5pm, the tour takes about 1.5-2 hours, and there is an admission charge.

Pall Mall is Bendigo's main boulevard, and has some of the city's grandest Victorian buildings. Take note of: the Italianate post office (1887) and law courts (1896); the Shamrock Hotel (1897); Alexandra Fountain (1881); the Beehive Store (1872); National Bank (1887) and Grand United HBS building (1886). Other buildings nearby include: the Bendigo Town Hall (1885); Bendigo Gaol (1864); Old Police Barracks (1859); St Paul's Cathedral (1868); Goldmines Hotel (1857); Specimen Cottage (1856).

View Street begins at the Alexandra Fountain, and also has some impressive 19th century buildings: Atkinson Building (1877); Bendigo Trades Hall (1885); Bendigo Art Gallery (1890); Capital Theatre (1874); Dudley House (1858); National Australia Bank (1863); Old Fire Station (1899); Rifle Brigade Hotel (1887); Sandhurst Trustees (1891).

Chinese Joss House, Finn Street, Emu Point, ℗5442 1685. The original Chinese temple was built in the 1860s of handmade bricks and timber, and painted red, the traditional Chinese colour for strength. To get there, follow the tram tracks towards Echuca, then turn at Lake Weeroona. The Joss House is operated by the National Trust, and is open daily 10am-5pm. Admission is adults ☻$3, children $1.

Golden Dragon Museum and Chinese Gardens, 5 - 13 Bridge Street, ℗5441 5044. Trace the history of Chinese influence in Bendigo, going right back to the gold rush days, in this impressive setting. Entry is ☻$7 adult, $4 child, and the complex is ⏱open daily 9.30am-5pm.

Vintage Talking Trams, 1 Tramways Avenue, ℗5442 2821. The Bendigo Trust has a collection of 34 vintage trams, and they are one of Bendigo's most popular tourist attractions. They run through the city centre, via Pall Mall, and along the 8km route between Central Deborah Mine and North Bendigo. A recorded commentary highlights more than 50 features along the way, and a stop at the Tram

Bendigo's Talking Trams

Museum in Tramways Avenue, ☏5442 2821, is included in the tour. The trams ⏱depart from Central Deborah Mine Mon-Fri 9.30am, 1 and 2pm, hourly on weekends and school and public holidays from 9.30am-4.30pm. The tour takes approximately one hour.

Hargreaves Mall is a retail shopping area in the city centre, and has a wide selection of specialty shops and boutiques.

Lake Weeroona, cnr Midland Highway & Nolan Street, is a delightful ornamental lake close to the city centre. Surrounded by trees and gardens, there are boat hire, picnic and barbecue facilities.

Discovery & Science Technology Centre, 7 Railway Place, ☏5444 4400, has hands-on exhibits and a vertical slide. Admission is ✪$7.50 adult, $4.50 child and it is ⏱open daily 10am-5pm.

Within a few minutes drive from the city centre there are many interesting places to visit -

Bendigo Pottery, Midland Highway, Epsom, ☏5448 4404, ⏱open daily 9am-5pm, with guided tours at 10.30am and 2.30pm. Admission is free.

Bendigo Market Place, 116 - 120 Mitchell Street, Bendigo, ☏5441 6906, ⏱open daily.

Kennington Reservoir, Reservoir Road, Bendigo - swimming, boating, windsurfing and canoeing. Barbecue and picnic grounds.

Espsom Market, off Midland Highway at Epsom past the Bendigo Pottery, ☏5448 8411, ⏱open every Sunday 8.30am-3pm. Country Victoria's largest undercover market.

Eaglehawk, an historic town 8km north-west of Bendigo, and the site of a gold rush in 1852.

One Tree Hill Lookout, 8km south of Bendigo - from the Fountain follow Mitchell Street, then Carpenter Street, into Spring Gully Road. Continue south and the turn-off is just before Tannery Lane.

Wineries in Bendigo include: *Balgownie Vineyards*, Hermitage Road, Maiden Gully, (8km west), ☏5449 6222, closed Sunday; *Chateau Leamon*, Calder Highway, Big Hill, 10km south of Bendigo, ☏5447 7995, closed Tuesday; *Chateau Dore Vineyard*, 8km southeast of Bendigo at Mandurang Valley, ☏5439 5278, closed Monday.

For information on other wineries in the surrounding districts, contact the Visitor Information Centre.

Castlemaine

Festivals

The Easter Fair has been staged for more than a century. The ten day festival commences with a street carnival on Easter Saturday, a 'waking of the dragon' ceremony takes place on Easter Sunday when a small lion wakes 'Sun Loong' with fireworks. Sun Loong is 100m long and is the largest known ceremonial Chinese dragon in the world. It is a colourful feature of the major procession on Easter Monday.

Facilites

Lawn bowls, ten-pin bowling, ice skating, roller skating, golf, tennis, swimming, croquet, indoor cricket, squash, horse racing and trotting and greyhound racing.

Outlying Attractions

Castlemaine

Nestling in a dip of the Great Dividing Range 38km (24 miles) south of Bendigo, Castlemaine is another gold mining town. Attractions in and around town include nineteenth-century Buda Historic Home & Garden in Hunter Street; Skydancers Butterfly Sanctuary on the Midland Highway, Harcourt; Kyirong Emu Farm on Strathlea Road, Strathlea; and Maldon Porcupine Township, a recreation of life in early Victoria, cnr Bendigo and Allan Roads, Maldon, ✆5475 1000.

The Castlemaine Visitor Information & Interpretive Centre is in Market Building, Mostyn Street, ✆5470 5566 or ✆1800 171 888.

Echuca-Moama

Population 9,000 and 2,500 respectively Echuca-Moama is located near the junction of the Murray, Campaspe and Goulburn Rivers, 205km (127 miles) from Melbourne.

Climate

Average daily temperatures: January max 32C (90F) - min 17C (63F); July max 15C (59F) - min 4C (39F). Average annual rainfall: 451mm (18 ins).

Characteristics

More than 130 years ago two ex-convicts, Henry Hopwood and James Maiden established the twin towns of Echuca-Moama on opposite sides of the Murray River. For about 40 years, from 1860 to 1900, Echuca was a busy port with hundreds of paddlesteamers and barges carrying supplies to stations along the Murray, Darling and Murrum-bidgee Rivers. Much of the romance of this era was captured in the television mini-series All The Rivers Run.

The name Echuca is Aboriginal for 'meeting of the water'.

How to Get There

By Bus
V/Line have a service from Melbourne on Tues, Wed, Thurs and Sat.
Greyhound Pioneer stop at Echuca on their Sydney/Adelaide run.

By Road
Echuca is near the junctions of the Murray Valley, Northern and Cobb Highways.

Accommodation

Echuca-Moama has motels, hotel/motels, a guest house, caravan parks, and self-contained unit accommodation. Here is a selection with prices for a double room per night, which should be used as a guide only. The telephone area code is 03.

Philadelphia Motel Inn, 340 Ogilvie Avenue (Murray Valley Hwy), 5482 5700. 24 units, licensed restaurant (closed Sunday), swimming pool, bbq - ✪$88-120.

Riverboat Lodge Motor Inn, 476 High Street, 5482 5777. 19 units, pool, spa - $90-115.

All Rivers Motor Inn, 115 Northern Highway, 5482 5677. 31 units, licensed restaurant (closed Sunday), pool, bbq - ✪$90-140.

Pevensey Motor Lodge, 365 High Street, 5482 5166. 20 units, pool, bbq - ✪$85-120.

Old Coach Motor Inn, 288 Ogilvie Avenue, 5482 3155. 19 units, pool, spa, bbq - ✪$65-115.

Big River Motel, 317 High Street, 5482 2522. 15 units, bbq - ✪$60-85.

Fountain Motel, 77 Northern Highway, 5482 3200. 13 units, pool, bbq - ✪$55-105.

Highstreet Motel, 439 High Street, 5482 1013. 11 units - ✪$60-70.

Pastoral Inn Hotel Motel, 100 Sturt Street, 5482 1812. 15 units, licensed restaurant - ✪$55-65.

Caravan Parks

Echuca Caravan Park, Crofton Street (Victoria Park), 5482 2157. (No pets allowed) - powered sites ✪$15-20 for two, on-site vans $35-45 for two.

Rich River Caravan Park, Crescent Street, 5482 3658. (No pets allowed) - powered sites ✪$15-25 for two, cabins $52-80 for two.

Yarraby Caravan Park, River Avenue, 5482 1533. (No dogs allowed) - powered sites ✪$15-20 for two, cabins (en-suite) $53-125 for two, cabins (standard) $40-53.

Riverlander Caravan Park, 48 Pianta Road, 5482 2558. (No pets allowed) - powered sites ✪$17 for two, cabins $47-90 for two.

For something different you could hire a houseboat from **Magic Murray Houseboats**, 5480 6099, or **Rich River Houseboats**, 5480 2444.

Eating Out

You can enjoy surprisingly fine dining in Echuca-Moama. The Tourism Centre has information on all the dining establishments in Echuca-Moama, and here we have a few names and addresses:

Oscar W's Wharfside, Red Gum Grill & Deck Bar, 101 Murray Esplanade, Echuca, 5482 5133 - popular and highly recommended restaurant, described by critics as Echuca's best.

Wistaria Tea Rooms, 51 Murray Esplanade, Echuca 5482 4210 - licensed - lunch, morning and afternoon teas, children welcome.

Top of the Town, High Street, Echuca, 5482 4600 - excellent quality fish and chips available from this take-away shop - open 7 days.

Fiori, 554 High Street, Echuca, 5482 6688 - licensed - Italian.

Cock 'n' Bull Restaurant, 17 Warren Street, Echuca, 5480 6988 - modern Australian - licensed - open 5.30pm Tue-Sat.

Riverview Estate Restuarant, 2 Merool Lane, Moama, 5480 0126 - riverside dining.

Radcliffe's, Radcliffe Street, Echuca, 5480 6720 - Mediterranean cuisine, licensed.

Giorgio's on the Port, 527 High Street Echuca, 5482 6117 - open every night for dinner - award-winning - authentic Italian food.

MV Mary Ann, 5480 2200 - licensed luxury cruising restaurant - lunch and dinner cruises.

(Map of northern Victoria and southern New South Wales showing towns including Swan Hill, Sea Lake, Woomelang, Birchip, Kerang, Quambatook, Gunbower, Deniliquin, Wanganella, Jerilderie, Lockhart, Urana, Finley, Oaklands, Mathoura, Berrigan, Tocumwal, Culcairn, Moama, Echuca, Cobram, Numurka, Kyabram, Shepparton, Charlton, Rochester, Wedderburn, Bridgewater on Loddon, Huntly, Elmore, Benalla, Nagambie, Euroa, Bendigo, Epsom, Maryborough, Ravenswood, Hume, Seymour, Castlemaine, Malmsbury, Ararat, Kyneton, Alexandra, Eildon, Clunes, Beaufort, Yea)

Echuca-Moama

Tourist Information

Echuca-Moama District Tourism is at 2 Heygarth Street, Echuca, ☏(03) 5480 7555 or 1800 804 446. They can be emailed at ✉emt@origin.net.au and the website is 👁www.echucamoama.com

Points of Interest

The **Port of Echuca**, ☏5482 4248, was once Australia's largest inland port, and the wharf, river boats, barges and century-old buildings have been restored. The Port is open daily and tickets for the Port Tours cost $10 adult and $6 child. A full ticket ($20 adult, $11 child), allows you to board the *Pevensey* (better known as the *Philadelphia* from *All The Riv-ers Run*) or the *Alexander Arbuthnot* which carries passengers during holiday periods and the last Sunday each month. *The Adelaide*, an historic logging boat, gives demonstration runs monthly, towing the D26 barge. Other features include a 10 minute film telling the Port story, an escape tunnel from the former cellar bar in the Star Hotel, the Paddle-steamer Gallery and the upstairs gallery in the Bridge Hotel.

The Historical Society Museum, opposite the Hopwood Gardens, has old River Charts, photographs, etc, and is ◷open weekends, Mon, Wed, public and school holidays 1-4pm, or by appointment, ☏5480 1325.

Echuca also has the **World in Wax Museum**, Australia's largest collection of wax figures by international artists, situated in the

High School. ☉Open daily 9am-5pm, ✆5482 3630.

There are one hour **cruises** on the *PS Canberra*, ✆5482 2711, and *PS Pride of the Murray*, ✆5482 5244. *MV Mary Ann* is a cruising restaurant that offers two hour luncheon and 3-4 hour dinner cruises. Also available is a river cruise for 2 day/nights aboard the *PS Emmylou*, ✆5482 4248.

Sharps Magic Movie House and Penny Arcade, opposite the Wharf, Bond Store, Port of Echuca, ✆5482 2361, have 30 penny arcade machines to play, the largest collection in Australia. You can also watch the old time movie

shows dating from 1890. ☉Open daily 9am-5pm.

The **Murray River Aquarium**, 640 High Street, ✆5480 7388, has fish and reptile displays.

Njernda, the Aboriginal Cultural Centre, is in the Old Court House in Law Place, ✆5482 3904, and has displays of local and traditional artifacts and videotapes/language tapes of the local area. For sale are traditional crafts by people descended from the Yorta Yorta and Wemba Wemba tribes. The Centre is ☉open daily, 10am-4.30pm.

Tisdall Winery is ☉open daily for tastings

The Murrray River

and cellar sales, Mon-Sat 10am-5pm, Sun 11am-5pm, ©5480 1349. It is in Murray Esplanade, one block from the Port of Echuca.

Visitors can enjoy a 'flutter on the pokies' (play the slot machines) at one of the 4 licensed clubs in Moama, which also have dining facilities.

Festivals

The Rotary Steam, Horse and Vintage Rally is held over the Saturday and Sunday of the Queen's Birthday weekend in June. It features working exhibits of Clydesdale horses, vintage and veteran vehicles and steam traction engines, allowing everyone to experience the sights and sounds of a by-gone era.

The Port of Echuca Heritage Steam Festival is staged over a weekend in late October. It is involves a cavalcade of riverboats and a fireworks display.

Facilities

Boating, bowls, bush walking, croquet, fishing, golf, horse racing, horse riding, sailing, swimming, trotting, water skiing, bingo, and bicycle and canoe hire are available.

The Barmah State Forest

Echuca-Moama

Outlying Attractions

Kyabram

Situated only 31km (19 miles) south-west of Echuca, Kyabram is becoming well known as an Arts and Crafts centre.

The Kyabram Fauna Park, 75 Lake Road, ☎5852 2883, is set in 55ha (128 acres) of pleasant natural surroundings, and has hundreds of Australian animals and birds which roam freely around the park. It also has a miniature railway, playground and kiosk, and is ⏱open daily 9.30am-5.30pm.

Rochester

The town of Rochester is 24km (15 miles) south of Echuca on the Northern Highway. It is the Hub of the North, and has palms, peppercorns, quaint shops and sleepy streets. Random House, situated in on the Campaspe River in Bridge Road, is a stately 19th cen-

tury homestead that has been restored to its former glory. It is ⏱open for morning and afternoon tea, Wed, Thurs, Fri and Sun. Meals and accommodation can be arranged by phoning ☎5484 1792.

The huge facility in the middle of town is the Devondale complex owned by the Murray Goulburn Co-operative Company. It is a major employer in the district, and has a retail store where you can sample and buy some of their products.

The Barmah Forest

The Forest is a 20 minute drive from Moama, and the Visitor Information Centre in Echuca has leaflets giving directions.

The Dharyna Centre, Sandridge Road, Barmah, ☎5869 3302, is a visitor centre also providing live-in educational opportunities for groups in the Barmah Forest, the largest Redgum Forest in the Southern Hemisphere.

Ballarat

Population 80,000

Ballarat is the main centre of the Victorian Central Highlands, which have a decidedly Scottish flavour to them. Ballarat was made famous through the Eureka Stockade, the bloody miners' rebellion in 1854.

The city is 113km (70 miles) from Melbourne, 985km (612 miles) from Sydney, 637km (396 miles) from Adelaide, and 747km (464 miles) from Canberra.

Characteristics

Over the years Ballarat has been known as 'The Goldfields', the 'Garden City', the 'City of Statues' and the 'Historical City', and it is all these and more.

The city is one of the best preserved in Australia, and also one of the most fascinating. Steeped in history, it is a monument to the pioneering adventurers who left their distant homelands in search of prosperity in the gold rush of the 1850s.

Incidentally, is it Ballarat or Ballaarat? The original spelling came from the aboriginal 'Ballaarat', meaning 'elbow place'. Over the years the second 'a' was dropped for convenience. In early 1990 the Ballaarat Council officially re-adopted the original spelling and it is now officially the City of Ballaarat, although for commercial or other purposes either spelling is acceptable.

How to Get There

By Bus

Greyhound Pioneer stop at Ballarat on their Melbourne/Adelaide/Perth and Melbourne/Adelaide/Alice Springs routes.

V/Line buses run from Melbourne to Ballarat, and the trip takes about two hours.

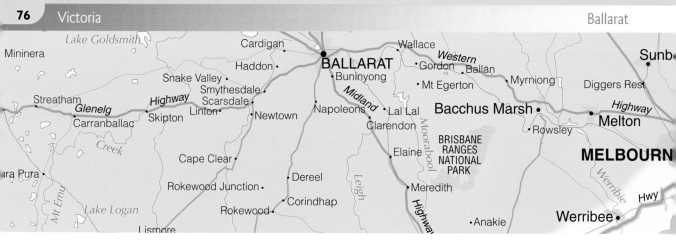

How to Get There - *Continued*

By Rail
There is a regular service Melbourne-Ballarat.
By Road
From Melbourne, via the four lane Western Freeway.

Tourist Information

Ballarat Tourist Information Centre is at 39 Sturt Street (cnr Albert Street), ©(03) 5320 5741 or ©1800 446 633. For further information email them at the address: ✉ tourism @ballarat.vic.gov.au or see the website 👁www.ballarat.com

Accommodation

Ballarat

Victoria's largest inland provincial city has a wide range of accommodation, and here we have a selection, with prices for a double room per night, which should be used as a guide only. ©The telephone area code is 03.

Mercure Inn Ballarat, 1845 Sturt St, ©5334 1600. 76 units, lic. restaurant, pool -✪$85-130.

Sundowner Chain Motor Inns, 312 Main Road, ©5331 7533. 25 units, licensed restaurant (closed Sun), pool, spa - ✪$95-150.

Park View Motor Inn, 1611 Sturt Street, ©5334 1001. 46 units, lic. restaurant, pool- ✪$75-100.

Ballarat Mid City Motor Inn, 19 Doveton Street North, ©5331 1222. 73 units, licensed restaurant (closed Sun), pool, sauna - ✪$100-125.

Begonia City Motor Inn, 244 Albert Street, Sebastopol, ©5335 5577. 15 units, swimming pool, bbq - ✪$85-110.

Ambassador Motel, 1759 Sturt Street, Alfredton, ©5334 1505. 22 units, licensed restaurant (closed Sun), swimming pool, spa, sauna, bbq - ✪$75-115.

City Oval Hotel/Motel, cnr Pleasant & Mair Streets, ©5332 1155. 8 units, licensed restaurant - ✪$64.
Caravan Parks
Ballarat and A Welcome Stranger Caravan Park, Cnr Water St & Scott Parade, ©5332 6818. (No pets allowed) - powered sites ✪$20 for two, cabins (en-suite) $62-94 for two, cabins (standard) $50-60 for two.

A Ballarat Windmill Caravan Park, Avenue of Honour, Western Highway, Alfredton, ©5334 1686. (No dogs) - powered sites ✪$25-30 for two, on-site vans $44 , cabins $60-120 for two.

Shady Acres Caravan Park, Melbourne Road (Western Hwy), ©5334 7233. (No dogs allowed) - powered sites ✪$18 for two, park cabins (en-suite) $60-72 for two, park cabins (standard) $25-35 for two.

Ballarat Goldfields Holiday Park, 108 Clayton Street, ©5332 7888. (No pets allowed) - powered sites ✪$21 for two, park cabins (en-suite) $65-70 for two.

Eating Out

As with any city of its size, Ballarat has a wide choice of restaurants, as well as those in the motels and hotels. Here are some names and addresses.

The Ansonia, 32 Lydiard Street, South Ballarat, ©5332 4678 - international cuisine - licensed - breakfast, lunch & dinner available.

Golden Crown Chinese Restaurant, cnr Main Road & Barkly Street, ©5332 2169 - ©open for lunch & dinner seven days - licensed & BYO - takeaway available.

Europa Cafe, 411 Sturt Street, ©5331 2486 - dishes in a variety of flavours - dinner Thu-Sat, breakfast & lunch daily - licensed.

Lillian's Restaurant, at the Sundowner Motor Inn, 312 Main Road, ©5331 7533 - modern Australian - good value - licensed.

The Bonshaw, cnr Tait Street & Ross Creek Road, ©5335 8346 - licensed, seafood/steak in candlelit atmosphere - mains under $20 - ©open Tues-Sat.

Peter Lalor Hotel, 331 Mair Street, ©5331 1702 - licensed, full a la carte menu and smorgasbord - ©open daily for lunch noon-2pm and dinner 6-8pm.

Boatshed Restaurant, 27 Wend-ouree Parade, ©5333 5533 - open seven days - situated beside Lake Wendouree.

Robin Hood Family Bistro, 33 Peel Street, ©5331 3348 - licensed, a la carte - ©open seven days with piano bar on Thurs, Fri and Sat nights.

Mexican Terrace Restaurant, 71 Victoria Street, ©5333 1435 - mexican, steak, vegetarian & children's menus - ©open Tue-Sun from 6pm - licensed.

Pancake Kitchen, Grenville Street, ©5331 6555 - BYO, family atmosphere.

There are also two branches of *McDonald's* in Ballarat.

Points of Interest

Gold was first discovered in the Ballarat area in 1851 by James Esmond, and the rush for gold was on. However, by the end of 1851, much of the surface gold had been depleted, and many diggers moved to the new fields at Bendigo and Castlemaine. Then, early in 1852, new arrivals from England (mainly Cornwall and Wales) heard that the gold had run out but decided to see for themselves. They dug to the Ordovician bedrock, and uncovered a veritable treasure trove. The rush was on again in earnest, with people coming from all over the world.

The government of the day had imposed a licence fee for the right to dig, and were more than happy with the revenue they received. However they didn't administer the system well, and there was the usual claim-jumping and skirmishes.

Tempers became short amongst the original miners, and the fields became a virtual tinder box. The spark that set it all afire came when a digger, James Scobie, was murdered, and a hotel owner named Bentley was charged with the crime, but found not guilty, contrary to popular belief. On the spot where Scobie had been murdered, about 5,000 diggers met, formed a committee, and held a meeting, which began in an orderly fashion, but soon degenerated, and the hotel was burnt to the ground. Several people were arrested, and although they were only given short terms of imprisonment, the incensed diggers formed the Ballarat Reform League with Peter Lalor as their leader.

The Governor listened to the grievances of the men, told them a franchise was being set up, and they returned to the diggings in a more reasonable state of mind - but not for long. An altercation between troopers and diggers caused many miners to burn their licenses in opposition to authority, thereby laying them-

Ballarat

Ballarat

selves open to conflict. Lalor and his men built a crude stockade of wagons, spikes, logs and slabs, and about 120 men were in this stockade, flying their own flag, on the night of December 2, 1854. The troopers attacked at dawn on the 3rd, and although the battle lasted barely twenty-five minutes, about 22 diggers and 6 soldiers were killed, and 114 prisoners were taken. The battle was lost, but the miners' rights improved as a consequence.

The **Eureka Stockade Centre**, cnr Rodier & Eureka Streets, 5333 1854, opened in March 1998 and cost $4 million to build. It involves a modern, interactive re-retelling of the story of the miner's brief but bloody uprising in 1854 Ballarat. The exhibition is well-done, and should be your first port of call to understand the city's past. It is open daily 9am-5pm, and entry is $8 adult, $4 child.

Opposite the exhibition is the **Eureka Memorial and Park**, near where the events actually occurred.

The **Ballarat Fine Art Gallery**, 40 Lydiard Street North, has the remains of the original Eureka Flag, depicting the Southern Cross, displayed in its own gallery alongside a changing display of related work. The flag was given to James Oddie, the gallery's founder and president, in 1895, by the widow of John King, a trooper who had taken part in the attack on the Stockade. The gallery was the first provincial art gallery to be established in Australia. The foundation stone for the present building was laid in 1887. It is open daily 10.30am-5pm. Admission is $4 adult, children free.

Historic Montrose Cottage, 111 Eureka Street, was built in 1856 and is the oldest remaining bluestone miner's cottage in Ballarat. Classified by the National Trust of Australia (Vic), the Cottage is also on the Australian Heritage List. It is open daily 9am-5pm, as is the adjacent **Eureka Museum**, which gives an insight into life on the goldfields, with an array of personal and household items dating from the 1850s. Outside is a cottage garden featuring old roses, herbs and other aromatic plants, and next door is Priscilla's Cottage, offering morning and afternoon teas and snacks. This is Ballarat's oldest attraction and a multi-award winner.

Ballarat Wildlife Park, cnr Fussel and York Streets, 5333 5933, is set in 15ha (37 acres) of parkland, and attractions include a large collection of Australian animals, barbecue and picnic areas, children's adventure playground, tropical reptile house, large salt water crocodiles, kiosk and wildlife souvenir shop, a cafe and takeaway food shop. The Park is open every day from 9am-5.30pm. Admission is $13.50 adult, $7.50 child, $38 family.

Blood on the Southern Cross is described as a "Night-time Sound and Light Spectacular". It is an unique and engaging re-creation of the Eureka Stockade, a turning point in Australia's history, which takes place on Soveriegn Hill (see opposite) - 5333 5777 for booking and information.

The **Gold Museum** is opposite Sovereign Hill in Bradshaw Street, and is run by the Ballarat Historical Society. The museum has a collection of rare gold coins, including a ducat, a denarius and a doubloon, and an exhibition of Chinese bronze and porcelain, watercolours, jewellery and clothing. There is also an historical pavilion with Aboriginal artefacts, relics of the wool industry, old signs and store fronts, bric-a-brac, and memorabilia of both Ballarat and Victoria. The Museum is open 9.30am-5.20pm daily.

The **Central Business District** of Ballarat is a treasury of architectural elegance - Lydiard Street has the 1872 Alexandria Tearooms, Old Colonists Hall (1887-89), former Mining Exchange (1888), Reid's Coffee Palace (1886 - now a private hotel), and the George Hotel, originally built in 1853 but the present building dates from 1903.

Sovereign Hill, in Bradshaw Street, 5331 1944, offers a trip back in time to the period of Ballarat's gold rush days. It is a re-created gold mining town complete with Main Street, busy with people in olden day dress and horse-drawn vehicles; a blacksmith; coach-builder; tinsmith; potter; furniture maker; Clarke Brothers' Grocery; the Apothecaries Hall; Spencer's Sweetshop; and the Hope Bakery. You can pan for gold, take a guided tour of the underground mine, play bowls at the Empire Bowling Saloon, or be photographed in period costume. There is something for everyone at Sovereign Hill, and plenty of places to eat or be entertained. The complex is open daily 10am-5pm. Entry is $25 adult, $12 child and $65 for families.

Botanical Gardens

Sturt Street has the Post Office (1863-1885), the Town Hall (1870), and a pagoda-like pavilion that was erected as a memorial to the bandsmen who played as the Titanic went down.

The Tourist Information Centre has information on other buildings of architectural merit.

At the western end of Sturt Street (Western Highway) is an unusual war memorial - the **Arch of Victory** and the **Avenue of Honour**. The Arch is across the highway, near the golf club, and is floodlit by night. Immediately west an avenue of around 4000 trees reaches to Lakes Burrembeet and Learmonth, each one bearing a name honouring one of the fallen.

The **Botanical Gardens** in Gillies Street are noted for the many specimens of mature trees ranging in age to over 120 years. About 46 of them have been registered on the National Trust register of Significant Trees. There is an informative free brochure on the gardens, that is available at most tourism outlets and accommodation, which lists the various attractions such as: Adventure Playground, the Avenue of Prime Ministers; the Begonia display (best in March); Lake Wen-douree; and the Tram Museum.

Lake Wendouree was originally called Yuille's Swamp, named after Archibald Yuille, who in turn had named his run Ballaarat after the local Aborigines. The Lake is the focus of recreation in Ballarat, with its beautiful gardens, boat sheds, shady trees and picnic spots. It was used in 1956 for the rowing events of the Olympic Games. There are ducks, swans and other water birds, and, as is the way these days, plenty of joggers. The swans are exceptionally friendly at most times, but can become quite feisty when they have cygnets with them, so take care.

The **Ballarat Tramway Museum** is operated by a volunteer group over an original section of track. The 1.3km of track began in 1887 as a horse-tramway, then the route was electrified in 1905 and officially closed in 1970-71. Rolling stock at the depot/museum includes 10 tramcars and horse tram No 1, and there is a photographic display. The trams run ⊙every weekend, public holidays and school holidays from 12-5pm, ©5334 1580.

The **Dinosaur World Fun Park & Fossil Museum**, Midland Highway, Creswick, ©5345 2676, is set in 12ha (30 acres) of bushland. 18 life-size dinosaurs and Model Land are features inside the complex. Ouside there are 36 picnic tables (many under cover), 16 barbecues, a takeaway kiosk, and plenty to see and do ⊙every day 9.30am-5pm.

The **Tuki Fishing Complex**, "Stoney Rises", Smeaton, ©5345 6233, is about 25 minutes from Ballarat, and you can hire all the necessary equipment and catch your trout for lunch. There are eight ponds and two lakes, all brimful with fish, and from the complex there are panoramic views over the Loddon Valley. ⊙Opening hours are daily 11am-6pm.

Kryal Castle is 8km (5 miles) east of Ballarat, off the Western Highway, and is ⊙open daily 9.30am-5.30pm, ©5334 7388. The castle occupies 2.4ha (6 acres) within a walled area, with 73 buildings, displays, museums, facilities and services. The castle opened in 1974, and is well worth visiting. There are gothic towers, turrets, parapets, battlements complete with moat, drawbridge, porticos, keep, tavern, craft shops, stables and dungeons. Live exhibitions include the 'Hanging of the Villain', 'Whipping of the Wench', and various changing shows. Whatever you do, don't miss the graveyard, and make sure you read the headstones. The Castle also has the *Golden Eagle Tavern*, where you can wine and dine like the knights of old. Entry is ✪$12.50 adult, $7.50 child.

Festivals

The Begonia Festival is held over 10 days in March, and is one Victoria's best known.

The Ballarat Agricultural Show is held on the Friday, Saturday and Sunday of the second weekend in November.

Facilities

Lawn bowls, croquet, fishing, gold panning, golf, greyhound racing, horse racing, rowing, sailing, squash, swimming, tennis and trotting.

Outlying Attractions

Clunes

Situated 40km (25 miles) north of Ballarat, Clunes was the first place where gold was discovered in Victoria. A small rush followed but no permanent development occurred until 1856. Commercial development began in 'Lower' Fraser Street in the 1860s, and by the 1870s, many of the fine civic buildings you see today were constructed. Mining ceased in the 1890s and a tree planting programme began, creating one of the prettiest small towns in Victoria.

The town has a museum, a motel, hotels, historic buildings, a supermarket, and a golf course. For more local information, contact the Clunes Museum on ©(03) 5345 3592.

Hepburn Springs

John Hepburn was credited with discovering the area in 1837, and he said it was the loveliest spot he had seen in his travels. He established an extensive sheep squat on Smeaton Hill (now Kooroocheang). The springs were known to the Aborigines of the area, and discovered by early settlers, but the true worth of their presence was overshadowed by the mining boom. However, when the gold ran out, the quality of the waters was found to equal that of Europe's famous health resorts, and soon attracted growing numbers to drink and bathe in the springs.

The Hepburn Spa Resort, Mineral Springs Reserve, has hot mineral water, herbal, mud, bubble and sinusoidal electric baths, and these are becoming the tourist mecca they were at the turn of the century, ©5348 2034.

Ballarat

Daylesford

John Egan first discovered gold at a site known as Wombat Flat Diggings, in August 1851. The township of Daylesford was surveyed and laid-out in 1854. A settlement, including Chinese market gardens, remained at the diggings site until 1929, when the area was flooded to create Lake Daylesford.

You will find the Daylesford Regional Visitor Information Centre in Vincent Street, ℰ(03) 5348 1339.

Maryborough

Situated 88km (55 miles) from Daylesford, Maryborough has a population of 8,500. It was occupied by graziers until 1854 when there was a gold rush to nearby White Hills, 5km to the north. By 1856, Maryborough's main street was a thriving thoroughfare serving some 50,000 diggers. By 1918, the gold had petered out, and secondary industry took over, making it one of the most highly indus-trialised towns in Australia. A town tour will give an insight into the town, and its historical attractions.

For more information, get in touch with the Central Goldfields Shire Office, 2 Neill Street, Maryborough, ℰ(03) 5461 0610, ✉email mail@ cgoldshire.vic.gov.au or visit ◉www .centralgoldfields.com.au

Avoca

This is another former mining town in the foothills of the Pyrenees Range at the junction of the Sunraysia and Pyrenees Highways, on the banks of the Avoca River. Its quiet hills teem with black wallabies and grey kangaroos, and there is a growing colony of koalas. The Pyrenees Tourist Association is at 122 High Street, ℰ(03) 5465 3767.

Wineries around Ballarat

Yellowglen Winery, Whites Road, Smythesdale, ℰ5342 8617 - ◷open Mon-Sat 10am-5pm, Sun noon-5pm.

Mount Avoca Vineyard, 45 minutes along the Sunraysia Highway from Ballarat, ℰ5465 3282 - ◷open Mon-Sat 10am-5pm, Sun from noon.

Redbank Winery, at the 200km post on Sunraysia Highway, ℰ5467 7255 - ◷open daily 9am-5pm.

The following wineries are open weekends and public holidays. For other times phone ℰ5368 7209..

Chepstowe Vineyard, Fitzpatricks Lane, Carngham, ℰ5344 9412.

Leura Glen Estate, 260 Green Gully Road, Glenlyon, ℰ5348 7785

Whitehorse Wines, 4 Reid Park Road, Mt Clear, ℰ5330 1719.

Ararat & The Grampians

Population 10,100
Ararat is situated near the Hopkins River, 203km (126 miles) north-west of Melbourne, in the central highlands of Victoria. It is the gateway to the Grampians.

Characteristics

The Ararat district was founded and settled around 1839-40 and gold was discovered in the area in 1854. Evidence of the extensive mining in the surrounding district still exists for the interested to see. The Municipality was declared a Borough in 1858, became a Town in 1934 and was declared a City in 1950.

Ararat is an important service centre for a rich farming and wine growing area. It boasts some of the finest agricultural and wine growing land in Victoria, and produces the State's top fine Merino wool, and has the largest sheep production in Australia.

Many visitors to the region use Ararat as a base to explore the magnificent natural resources in the Mount Cole Forest Ranges and the popular Grampians National Park.

How to Get There

By Bus
Greyhound Pioneer call into Ararat on their Melbourne/Adelaide runs.
By Train
Ararat is connected by rail with Geelong, Portland, western, north western and central Victoria.
By Road
Ararat is on the Western Highway, 545km (339 miles) from Adelaide and 203km (126 miles) from Melbourne.

Accommodation

Ararat has motels, hotels and caravan parks. Following is a selection, with prices for a double room per night, which should be used as a guide only. ✆The telephone area code is 03.

Ararat Colonial Lodge & Pyrenees Restaurant, 6 Ingor Street, ✆5352 4644. 19 units, unlicensed restaurant, pool, bbq - ✪$90-105.

Statesman Motor Inn, Western Highway, ✆5352 4111. 19 units, licensed restaurant - ✪$85-100.

Ararat Central Motel, 249 Barkly Street, ✆5352 2255. 22 units, unlicensed restaurant, swimming pool - ✪$65.

Mount Ararat Motor Inn, 367 Barkly Street, ✆5352 2521. 9 units, bbq, playground - ✪$60.

Chalambar Motel, 132 Lambert Street, ✆5352 2430. 10 units, bbq, playground - ✪$45.

Caravan Parks

Acacia Caravan Park, 6 Acacia Avenue, ✆5352 2994. (Pets allowed by arrangement) - heated pool, powered sites ✪$16 for two, on-site vans $33-42 for two, cabins (en-suite) $55-90 for two, cabins (standard) $35-50 for two.

Pyrenees Caravan Park, 67 Pyrenees Highway, ✆5352 1309. (Pets allowed at manager's discretion) - powered sites ✪$16 for two, on-site vans $30-50 for two, cabins $55-80.

Eating Out

There is not a wide range of choices in Ararat, but the following provide good meals at reasonable prices, and will give you an idea of what is on offer.

Man Hing Chinese Restaurant, 190 Barkly Street, ✆5352 3311 - BYO - lunch Mon-Sun 12-2pm, Dinner Sun-Thurs 5-10pm, Fri-Sat 5-11pm.

Noble Garden Restaurant, 204 Barkly Street, ✆5352 2019.

Sicilian's Bar & Restaurant, 102 Barkly Street, ✆5352 2627.

Vines Cafe & Bar, 74 Barkly Street, ✆5352 1744.

Statesman Motor Inn, Western Highway, ✆5352 4111.

Ararat RSL Club, 76 High Street, ✆5352 2794.

Tourist Information

Ararat and Grampians Visitor Information Centre, 91 High Street, ✆(03) 5355 0281 or ✆1800 657 158. Email ✎tourinfo@ararat.vic.gov.au or visit 👁www.ararat.asn.au

There is also the Ararat Tourist Information Centre in Barkly Street, ✆(03) 5352 2096.

Points of Interest

The town was named by the first settler, Horatio Spencer Wills, who set off in a covered wagon with 5,000 sheep from the Murrum-bidgee area in NSW, to a grazing site near the Grampian Mountains. After 11 months of travel, in March 1840, Wills rested on a large bald mountain, noted that he was only one day's travel from his destination, and called the mountain 'Mount Ararat' for as he said, "Like the Ark, we rested here".

Ararat has many historical buildings classified by the National Trust, and the Tourist Information Centre has a brochure setting out a City Area Walk which takes in the splendid architecture of yesteryear. It commences at the **Art Gallery**, on the corner of High & Vincent Streets, open Mon-Fri 11am-4pm, Sat closed (except school holidays 12-4pm), Sun 12-4pm. You then visit the **Town Hall**, which incorporates the Arts Centre; the Shire Hall; the **Langi Morgala Museum** (open Sat-Sun 2-4pm); the **YMCA**; the **Mural** by Artist Hugh Anderson in High Street; **Pyrenees House**; the **Old Gaol**; **Alexandra Gardens**; the **Old Post Office and Sub Treasury**; the **Court House**; the **Edith Cavell Memorial**; and a **Grapevine** that has survived since 1856 when it was planted by G.W.H. Grano. The walk can take from 1/2 hour to 2 hours, depending on how much time you spend at each stop.

The Information Centre also has three **Driving Tours from Ararat**, which travel a bit further afield, and apart from the places visited on the walk, visit the following: One Tree Hill scenic lookout; McDonald Park approximately 4km from city centre; Copes Hill scenic view; Cathcart Ridge Winery 5352 1997; Carrol's Cutting with views to the Grampians; Pinky Point where gold was first found; Norval Dam for fishing, swimming and yabbying; Montara Winery 5352 3868; and Green Hill Lake.

Green Hill Lake, 4km from the city centre, is stocked with perch, trout and yellowbelly. There are gas barbecues, shade shelters, adult playground equipment and a boat ramp. The lake also has canoe channels and islands.

Alexandra Gardens have a Fernery and Glass House, which is used for growing orchids, and in fact, Ararat is known as the orchid centre of the west and has an annual orchid display in the town hall during October.

Ararat has eight district **wineries**, with most open for cellar sales and tastings. The Seppelts guided tour is a highlight of a visit to the area. Tours are Mon-Sat 10.30am, 1.30pm and 3pm and the cellar door is open 10am-5pm Mon-Sun, 5361 2239.

Festivals

The Great Western Vintage Races are held on the Australia Day weekend in January.

Ararat Highland Sports, featuring the Ararat Gift (foot race) are held on the Labour Day Weekend in March.

Golden Gateway Festival is over ten days in October.

Facilities

Lawn bowls, croquet, horse racing, trotting, swimming, tennis and squash.

Outlying Attractions

Mount Cole Forest
The Forest straddles the Great Dividing Range about 20km (12 miles) east of Ararat. Mount Cole and Mount Lonarch Forests are excellent examples of forests resulting from multi-use management, and in area total about 12,150ha (30,010 acres). They produce a steady supply of high quality milling timbers to local sawmills, while providing wildlife

Rockclimbing in the Grampians

habitat and recreational opportunities. The area also has another important value as its timbered slopes act as catchments for the streams that supply water to neighbouring towns. Road surfaces throughout the forest are good, but narrow, and allowances for slower speeds should be made.

Mount Cole Forest has become one of the most popular spots in Australia for Hang Gliding enthusiasts to practise. There are three sites used for take-off – Ben Nevis, Mt Buangor and Mt Langi Ghiran. While you might not be interested in jumping off a mountain yourself, it is exciting to watch others risking life and limb.

For those interested in nature, the things to look out for are: wild-flowers, including Rare Grevillea; kangaroos and wallabies; platypus (experts guarantee they are around in the streams, but don't get your hopes too high); echidnas, koalas, deer, tree ferns, waterfalls.

Grampians National Park

The Grampians became Victoria's largest National Park on July 1, 1984.

The start of the Park is about 25km (15 miles) from Ararat, west of the township of Moyston. There are several ways to enter the Park from Moyston, through Pomonal to Hall's Gap, or west from Moyston to Mafeking and Mt William. The Park consists of 167,000ha (412,490 acres) and has a rich variety of native flora, wildlife, and Aboriginal rock art sites. The eastern slopes of the Grampians present some of the most beautiful scenery in the area with an abundance of heath, wildflowers and the tall eucalypt forest with the red gum woodland in Victoria Valley a special feature.

The Park supports over 860 native plant species. Kangaroos, koalas, echidna, possums and gliders are common, and over 200 bird species have been recorded.

More information on the Grampians is available from Parks Australia, ✆131 963 or by dropping into the information centre on Dunkeld Road near Halls Gap, ✆5356 4381.

West of Moyston, about 20km (12 miles) is the Mafeking Reserve where the 'discovery of gold' Cairn is located depicting the site of the 1900 gold rush to the area. It is reported that over 7000 miners were in the area then, and today you can still see the sluiced gullies and disused shafts. Special care should be taken in the area, as the shafts can be dangerous.

The Mount William picnic area on the eastern slopes of the Grampians is a delightful spot, with the Kalymna Falls a short walking distance away.

The main wildflower season is in Spring (September-November), but Autumn is also a popular time to visit.

Great Western

Midway between Ararat and Stawell is the little township of Great Western, which gives its name to fine wines, including the champagne-style Great Western Special Reserve, which matures in the cellars beneath the sloping hills of Seppelts vineyards. There are many wineries in the town, all offering cellar door sales and tastings, and information can be obtained from the Tourist Information Centre in Stawell.

Stawell

A former gold mining town 30km (19 miles) west of Ararat, Stawell is probably better known now for the Stawell Gift, the world's richest professional foot running race. It is held for 3 days over the Easter break, and is a handicap race over 120m (131 yds). Since 1986, the carnival has been open to professional and amateurs, and attracts top Australian and international competitors. In Lower Main Street is the Stawell Gift Hall Of Fame, with videos, photographs and equipment covering over a century of history, ✆open Wed-Sun 10am-4pm, or by appointment, ✆5358 1326.

The Stawell & Grampians Tourism Information Centre is at 54 Western Highway, ✆(03) 5358 2314, and is ⏰open Mon-Fri 9am-5.30pm, Sat-Sun 9.30am-5pm. From the office you can get a brochue which shows visitors the attractions of Stawell.

The Walk starts in Stawell's 'World in Miniature' in London Road, ✆5358 1877. This Tourist Park features a unique presentation of world cultures, and Australian and local history displayed in dioramas and working models, both indoor and outdoors in landscaped gardens. You might also like to stroll through the Historic Precinct, and the Visitor Centre will guide you.

Halls Gap

Halls Gaps is the heart of the Grampians National Park in the picturesque Fyans Valley. The township offers a variety of accommodation, a comprehensive shopping centre and facilities including tennis courts, swimming pool, restaurants, horse riding, walks, scenic 4WD tours, golf course, fun park, nurseries, nearby wildlife park, winery and National Park visitor centre, ✆5356 4381.

The sandstone ranges of the Grampians National Park surround Halls Gap, providing views of rugged escarpments and a tranquil atmosphere. The ridges and valleys are filled with Australian fauna, wildflowers, treefern gullies, strange rock formations, Aboriginal rock art, crystal clear rock pools, and many waterfalls, such as McKenzie Falls *(pictured left)*.

Mildura

Population 19,360
Mildura is situated on the Murray River at the junction of the Sturt, Silver City and Calder Highways. It lies 560km (348 miles) from Melbourne, 398km (247 miles) from Adelaide, 1068km (664 miles) from Sydney, and 780km (485 miles) from Canberra.

Climate

Mildura has a dry, mild winter climate and 400 hours more sunshine each year than Surfers Paradise in Queensland. The average summer temperature is 32C (90F) with most days around 29C (84F).

Characteristics

The north-west of Victoria is known as Sunraysia, and Mildura is the main town. It is a great place to relax as well as being the threshold of the great outback, which begins just beyond the far banks of the Murray. Mildura is called 'The Oasis in the Desert', with mile upon mile of lush, productive vineyards and orchards, in the midst of dry, harsh Mallee country.

How to Get There

By Air
Mildura has a budy regional airport, ©5022 2777 for information on flight services and schedules.
By Bus
V/Line and Greyhound Pioneer have daily services from capital cities.
By Rail
The Vinelander from Melbourne daily except Saturday (overnight 10 hours). V/Line services the region daily.

Mildura

Accommodation

Mildura has plenty of motels, hotels guest houses, serviced apartment buildings and caravan parks/camping grounds. Here is a selection, with prices for a double room per night, which should be used as a guide only. The telephone area code is 03.

Chaffey International Motor Inn, 244 Deakin Avenue, 5023 5833. 32 units, licensed restaurant (closed Sun), pool, spa - ✪$100-175.

City Colonial Motor Inn, 24 Madden Avenue, 5021 1800. 14 units, bbq, pool - ✪$75-105.

Sandors Motor Inn - Mildural, 179 Deakin Avenue, 5023 0047. 30 units, licensed restaurant, swimming pool - ✪$100-105.

City Gate Motel, 89 Seventh Street, 5022 1077. 22 units, bbq, pool, spa - ✪$70-90.

Mildura Grand Hotel, Seventh Street opposite the railway station, 5023 0511. 108 rooms, licensed restaurant, bistro, swimming pool, spa, sauna - ✪$110-143.

Mildura Park Motel, 250 Eighth Street, 5023 0479. 28 units, bbq, pool - ✪$50-100.

Orana Motor Inn, 2101 Calder Highway, Irymple, 5024 5903. 12 units, swimming pool - ✪$50-70.

Caravan Parks

Golden River Caravan Gardens, Flora Avenue, 5021 2299. (No dogs allowed) - powered sites ✪$20 for two, cabins (en-suite) $50-130 for two, cabins $50 for two.

Cross Roads Holiday Park, cnr Deakin Avenue & Fifteenth Street, 5023 3239. (No pets allowed) - powered sites ✪$19-20 for two, cabins (en-suite) $50-100 for two.

Sunraysia Holiday Park, cnr Walnut Avenue & Sturt Highway, 5023 1914. (No pets) - powered sites ✪$15 for two, cabins $ 40-60 for two.

Desert City Tourist and Holiday Park, Calder Highway, 5021 1533. (No pets allowed) - powered sites ✪$15-22 for two, cabins (en-suite) $40-86 for two, cabins (standard) $40-90.

House Boats

For a holiday with a difference, get a few friends together and hire a houseboat, to cruise down the mighty Murray. The boats range from 6 berth to 12 berth units, from budget price to luxuriously equipped top of the range. For further information on this alternative accommodation, contact the Mildura Visitor Information & Booking Centre, (03) 5021 4424, or one of the following:

Adventure Houseboats, Sturt Highway, Buronga, 5023 4787.

Mildura Holiday Houseboats, 842 Fifteenth Street, Mildura, 3502, 5021 4414.

Sunraysia Houseboats, 48 Wentworth Street, 5027 3621.

Sunseeker Houseboats, 189 Game Street, Merbein, 3502, 1800 035 529 (free call).

How to Get There - *Continued*

By Road
From Adelaide by the Stuart Highway.
From Sydney by the Mid-Western Highway.
From Melbourne by the Calder/Sunraysia Highway.

Tourist Information

The Mildura Visitor Information & Booking Centre is located at 180 -190 Deakin Avenue, (03) 5021 4424 or 1800 039 043 (bookings). Additionally, you can email them at ✉ tourism@mildura.vic. gov.au or explore the website at 👁 www.milduratourism.com

Eating Out

Whether you prefer French, Italian, Mexican, Chinese or Vegetarian, a la carte, bistro, or casual, Mildura has the restaurant to suit your taste, and your pocket. Here is a selection:

Doms Tavern Restaurant, 28 Langtree Avenue, ©5021 3822 - open Mon-Sat, 6-30pm till late. Upstairs is the Carlyle Night Club, open Thurs, Fri and Sat, 9pm-3am.

Rendezvous Restaurant, 34 Lang-tree Avenue, ©5023 1571 - French cuisine, with bistro and wine bar - open for lunch Mon-Fri, dinner Mon-Sat.

Mildura Settlers, 110-114 Eighth Street, 5023 0474 - open Mon-Wed 8.30am-midnight, Thu-Sat 8.30am-2am - modern Australian - licensed.

Fasta Pasta, 30 Langtr ee Avenue, ©5022 0622.

Reef & Beef Restaurant, Deakin Avenue, ©5023 5023.

Marias Pizza & Pasta Palace, 210a Deakin Avenue, ©5023 7713.

Belvue Restaurant, at the Commodore Motor Inn, cnr Deakin Avenue & 7th Street, ©5023 0241.

Regal Chinese Restaurant, 224 Deakin Avenue, ©5021 3688.

Barneys Seafood Restaurant, 360 Deakin Avenue, ©5021 2166.

Dragon Tower Chinese Restaurant, 29 Langtree Avenue, ©5023 1925.

Wirraway Bistro, 130 Madden Avenue, ©5023 1187.

Dom's Tavern Restaurant, 28 Langtree Avenue, ©5021 3822.

Bel-Jardin Restaurant, 376 Deakin Avenue, ©5023 7377.

And, of course, we can't forget *McDonald's*. The local branch is at 395 Deakin Avenue, ph 222 544.

Points of Interest

In 1885, Alfred Deakin, the then Premier of Victoria, persuaded Canadian brothers, George and William Benjamin Chaffey to help plan Mildura. It was laid out in an American grid pattern, and most of its streets were given numbers instead of names. The Chaffeys installed pumps to lift water from the Murray, and after some initial problems with salt pollution, the area became well known for its fruit. Much of Mildura's history is preserved in the **Museum of Local History**, which is housed in Rio Vista, the stately home of W.B. Chaffey in Cureton Avenue - open 6 days. Also there is the **Mildura Arts Centre**, one of the best provincial galleries in Australia, ©5018 8330.

Dolls on the Avenue is a collection of hundreds of dolls from every decade, and is ⊙open daily 10am-4pm. It is in Benetook Avenue, ⊘5025 7113.

Golden River Zoo, 4km from Mildura on the banks of the Murray River is a fine privately owned zoo. Open daily 9am-5pm on Flora Avenue, off 11th Street. For information on animal show times ⊘5023 5540. Entry is $12 adults, $6 children.

Woodsie's Gem Shop is Australia's largest jewellery manufacturing complex, and one of Mildura's top attractions. It comprises: a workshop open to visitors; a spectacular showroom where finished items are for sale; an Aladdin's Cave full of glowing rocks and glittering crystals; a Crazy Maze with 100 different species of creepers over an acre of land to test your skill; and a Cave-Inn Cafeteria. The complex is on the corner of Morpung and Cureton Avenues, Nichols Point, 6km from Mildura, ⊘5024 5797. It is ⊙open daily 9am-5.30pm, and there is a modest admission fee to the Cave and Maze Section. The rest of the complex is free.

Orange World, 7km from Mildura on the Silver City Highway, is a fully operational citrus property with: ⊙Tours on Tractor Train, 10.30am and 2.30pm; Citrus Tour; Red Emperor Tour, including a tour of Stanley Winery, 11.30am. Tours run daily, with extra tours during school holidays. For further information ⊘5023 5197.

River Cruises

You can experience the old river boat era when you sail down the Murray on a paddleboat, and there are plenty of day and half-day cruises available. Details of current sailings are provided on notice-boards on Mildura Wharf, but here are a few examples.

PS Melbourne, ⊘5023 2200, the only original steam driven Paddle-steamer (built 1912) ⊙departs Mildura Wharf 10.50am and 1.50pm for a 2 hr cruise, which goes through Lock 11.

PV Loyalty, 5027 3224, has daily cruises (except Saturdays) on the Darling River, ⊙departing from behind Wentworth Services Club at 1.45pm (returns 3.45pm).

PV Rothbury specialises in day cruises, including lunch. Cruise to the Golden River Zoo ⊙leaves 9.50am on Wednesdays, and returns 3pm. Cruise to Trentham Estate Winery, leaves 10.30am Thursdays and returns 3.30pm. There are additional cruises during school holidays. The boat is also available for charter day or night cruises, ⊘5023 2200.

Facilities

Olympic swimming pool, 12th Street; putt putt golf course, cnr 7th Street and Orange Avenue; ten pin bowling, King Avenue; old time dance at Nichols Point Hall, ph 232 208, Saturday 8pm-midnight; tennis, golf, lawn bowls, squash, skating, boating, water skiing, fishing, croquet, and badminton.

Outlying Attractions

Red Cliffs

15km (9 miles) south of Mildura along the Calder Highway on the way to Melbourne, lies the town of Red Cliffs which is currently enjoying a surge in development. The town gets its name from the nearby striking red cliffs which dominate the Murray River. In the early 1890s, George Chaffey bought 6060ha (15,000 acres) of rich mallee land above the cliffs to grow vines, but the cliffs proved too steep for pumping irrigation water, and it was not for another 30 years that prosperity reached the town. That was when more than 700 soldiers were re-settled in the area after World War I, and today the area is an important part of the citrus and dried fruits industries.

Using Red Cliffs as a base, the visitor has a great variety of attractions to see, ranging from the huge Southcorp Karadoc Winery, to vari-

Paddleboat on the Murray River

ous handcraft, art and gemstone displays. In the heart of the town, in Barclay Square, is Big Lizzie, the largest traction engine ever built in Australia, which took two years to make the journey from Melbourne.

Hattah-Hulkyne National Park
Murray-Kulkyne National Park

This vast Mallee park is about 70km (43 miles) south of Mildura and provides striking contrasts teeming with birdlife, kangaroos, emus and colourful wildflowers. The park information centre can be reached from the Calder Highway turn-off at Hattah (look for the store) - also enter through Nangiloc/Colignan, ✆13 1963.

Mungo National Park

The Park contains the unique Walls of China, a range of dunes up to 46m (150 ft) high shaped by erosion into a barrier 27km (17 miles) long, leaving a foreground likened to a lunar landscape, or part of the Sahara Desert. Many geological and archaeological discoveries have been made in the area, and Aboriginal ovens can be seen. There is also an old shearing shed, built by Chinese labourers more than a century ago. The site is about 110km (68 miles) north-west of Mildura, on a dry weather road. Phone ✆5029 7292 for more information.

Wentworth

The historic town of Wentworth NSW, is situated where the Darling River joins the Murray, and is a 20 minute drive from Mildura. The Wentworth Tourist Information Centre, 66 Darling Street, ✆5027 3624, is ⏰open seven days a week (9.30-4p, Mon-Fri and 10am-2pm on weekends), and will provide details of scenic attractions. You can email them at ✉tourism@ wentworth.nsw.gov.au or visit the website ☞www.wentworth.nsw. gov.au

One site that you must not miss is the Old Wentworth Gaol, 1879-1927, in Beverley Street. It was designed to serve a vast outback region, and now stands as a vivid reminder of those harsh and uncompromising days when Wentworth stood on the edge of the lonely Australian inland. Classified as essential to the preservation of Australia's heritage, the gaol is a tribute to the craftsmanship of the pioneer builders and to the unfortunate inmates. The gaol also houses the Nanya Exhibit, dedicated to the courage and ingenuity of a remarkable man, and the beautiful Morrison collection. ⏰Open daily 10am-5pm, ✆5027 3337.

A walk through town will take you past quaint and notable buildings, some of whch are heritage listed. After visiting the Old Wentworth Gaol, stop in at the Museum, also in Beverly Street, for its fascinating fossil collection.

Wineries

Capogreco Wines, Riverside Avenue between 17th and 18th Streets, South Mildura. ⏰Tastings, sales and inspections Mon-Sat 10am-6pm, ✆5022 1431.

Southcorp Winery, Karadoc. Guided tours Mon-Fri 11am, 2pm and 3.3-pm. ⏰Tastings and sales Mon-Fri 9am-5pm, Sat 10am-4.30pm, ✆5051 3333.

Mildara Blass Winery, Wentworth Road, Merbein. ⏰Guided tours Mon-Fri aa1m, 2pm, 3.30pm. Tastings and sales Mon-Fri 9am-5pm, Sat 11am-4pm, Sunday noon-4pm, ✆5025 2303.

Buronga Hill Winery, Silver City Highway, Buronga. ⏰Tastings and sales Mon-Fri 9am-5pm, Sat 10.30am-4pm, Sun noon-4pm. Winery tours by appointment, ✆5022 5100.

Trentham Estate Winery, Sturt Highway, Trentham Cliffs. ⏰Tastings and sales Mon-Fri 9am-5pm, Sat-Sun 10am-5pm, ✆5024 8888.

Mildura

Warrnambool

Population 28,000
Warrnambool is situated on the coast, 263km (163 miles) south-west of Melbourne, where the Princes Highway meets the Great Ocean Road.

Climate

Average temperatures: January max 23C (73F) - min 13C (55F); July max 14C (57F) - min 6C (43F). Average hours of sunshine: summer 8, autumn 4, winter 3, spring 5. Wettest six months May-October.

Characteristics

Warrnambool was popular with the old whalers and sealers but due to reduced hunting, Warrnambool is now visited each year by a herd of the rare Southern Right whales, and a viewing platform has been erected at Logan's Beach to enable visitors to obtain a better view of the whales, which usually remain in the area for several weeks.

How to Get There

By Bus
Greyhound Pioneer, ©13 2030, stop at Warrnambool on the Melbourne/Adelaide coastal route.

By Rail
There is a regular V/Line service between Melbourne and Warrnambool, ©13 6196.

By Road
From Melbourne, travel to Geelong and then take the Princes Highway if in a hurry, but if you have more time, then take one of Australia's really beautiful roads, the Great Ocean Road which follows the coast.

Warrnambool is 263km (163 miles) from Melbourne via the Princes Highway, 211km (131 miles) from Mt Gambier, and 654km (406 miles) from Adelaide.

NORTH

0   15   30 km

Accommodation

Warrnambool

Here is a selection of accommodation, with prices for a double room per night, which should be used as a guide only. The phone area code is 03.

Guthrie Heights Apartment, 8/148 Merri Street, 5562 1600. 1 unit, 3 queen ensuites, sea views, barbecue - ✪$160.

Warrnambool Heritage Cottage, 26 MacDonald Street, 5562 6531. Private courtyard, barbecue - ✪$120-160.

Sundowner Chain Motor Inn, 525 Raglan Parade, 5562 3866. 60 units, licensed restaurant, swimming pool, spa - ✪$110-200.

Tudor Motel Warrnambool, 519 Raglan Parade, 5562 8877. 22 units, licensed restaurant (closed Sunday off-season), spa - ✪$100-150.

Olde Maritime Motor Inn, cnr Merri & Banyan Streets, 5561 1415. 37 units, licensed restaurant, spa - ✪$90-170.

Western Coast Motel, 349 Raglan Parade, 5562 2755. 21 units, restaurant - ✪$80-120.

Warrnambool Gateway Motor Inn, 69 Raglan Parade, 5562 8622. 26 units, Quigley's licensed restaurant (closed Sunday), barbecue, heated swimming pool - ✪$90-125.

Warrnambool Hotel, cnr Koroit & Keppler Streets, 5562 2377. 16 rooms, a la carte restaurant - ✪$70 including breakfast.

Motel Downtown Warrnambool, 620 Raglan Parade, 5562 1277. 58 units, heated swimming pool, spa - ✪$70-200.

Western Hotel, cnr Timor & Kepler Streets, 5562 2011. 20 units, standard facilities - ✪$60.

Bed and Breakfast

Merton Manor B&B, 62 Ardlie Street, 5562 0720. 6 rooms, barbecue - ✪$150-170.

Casa D'Oro B&B, 42 Shady's Lane, 5565 4243. 3 rooms, barbecue, comfortable rooms - ✪$90.

Whalesway, 6 Florence Street, 5661 2660. 2 rooms, barbecue - ✪$75-80.

Caravan Parks

Ocean Beach Holiday Village, Pertobe Road, 5561 4222. 58 sites, 26 cabins, no pets, barbecue, heated pool - powered sites ✪$22-30 for two, cabins $60-110 for two.

Warrnambool Holiday Park, cnr Raglan Parade & Simpson Street, 5562 5031. 17 sites, 17 cabins, no dogs, barbecue, heated pool - powered sites ✪$20-26, cabins $60-85.

Fig Tree Holiday Village, 33 Lava Street, 5561 1233. 72 sites, 23 cabins, no pets, barbecue - powered sites ✪$17-30 for two, cabins $55-90.

Caravarna Lodge, 81 Henna Street, 5562 3376. 42 sites, 4 cabins, barbecue, heated pool - powered sites ✪$14-17 for two, on-site vans $25-40 for two, cabins $30-50.

Hostels

Warrnambool Beach Backpackers, 17 Stanley Street, 5562 4874. 6 rooms, cooking facilities, guest dining - ✪$15.

Backpackers Barn, 90 Lava Street, 5562 2073. 15 rooms, cooking and dining - ✪$14.

Eating Out

There are over 50 places to have a meal in Warrnambool, from cafes to quality restaurants, and the Tourist Information Office will have details. Here is a selection.

Balenas Cafe, 158 Timor Street, ℰ5562 0900. Contemporary Australian cuisine as well as seafood and steaks with Italian, Mediterranean and International influences. Open 7 days.

Jukes Cafe Restaurant, 525 Raglan Parade, ℰ5562 3866. A-la-carte menu with entertainment on Saturday evening. Licensed, open seven days for breakfast and dinner.

Oriental Restaurant, 80-82 Liebig Street, ℰ5562 7079. BYO, Chinese and Australian fare, lunch and dinner, open 7 days.

Mahogany Ship, 91 Merri Street, ℰ5561 3866. Australian seafood steak and pasta is served in this Scottish themed restaurant. A-la-carte dining with sea views.

Bojangles, 61 Liebig Street, ℰ5562 8751. Award-winning Italian restaurant offering wood-fire pizzas and pastas as a specialty. Licensed, open for dinner only.

Beach Babylon, 72 Leibig Street, ℰ5562 3714. Seafood with Mediterranean and Australian flavours. Open every day.

Restaurant Malaysia, 69 Liebig Street, ℰ5562 2051. Also has Thai, Indian and Chinese dishes, BYO, open 7 days, noon-2pm, 6pm to late. Yum Cha, Sun noon-2pm.

Freshwater, 78 Leibig Street, ℰ5561 3188. Licensed restaurant serving modern Australian and International cuisine and offering local wines.

The Blues, 142 Timor Street, ℰ5562 2033. Family oriented dining with live local music. Australian seafood and steaks.

Images, Liebig Street, ℰ5562 4208. Licensed restaurant with a family atmosphere.

Breakers, 79 Banyan Street, ℰ5561 3088. All types of seafood served in an Australian style.

Clovelly, cnr Banyan & Merri Streets, ℰ5561 1415. A-la-carte menu with seafood, steak, pasta.

Dragon Inn, 219 Lava Street, ℰ5562 1517. Chinese cuisine.

Visitor Information

The Tourist Information Office is at 600 Raglan Parade, ℰ(03) 5564 7837, and it is ⏱open daily 9am-5pm, or you can email the manager at the email address: ✉nan_adams @wcc.mav.asn.au. The website to visit is 👁www. warrnambool.org

In addition, Shipwreck Coast Tourism can be found at 174a Timor Street, ℰ5561 7894.

Points of Interest

Flagstaff Hill Maritime Museum, Merri Street, ℰ5564 7841, recreates the atmosphere of an early Australian coa-stal port. The lighthouse and associated buildings, and the 1887 fortifications are the original features of the site, and around them the village has been created. The story of shipping and the sea unfolds for visitors as they tour the village. Each building portrays an important aspect of port life in the last century, whether it be the role of the Ship Chandler or the function of the Mission to Seamen Church. Among the relics on display there is the Loch Ard peacock: an 1851 Minton porcelain statue which was washed up (still in its packing case) in Loch Ard Gorge after a ship-wreck. The museum is ⏱open daily 9.00am-5.00pm, adults ✪$9.50, child $4.50, pensioner $8, family $26.

Lake Pertobe Park has causeways, walking tracks, a maze, a flying fox, paddle boats and a well-equipped Adventure Playground behind the surf beach of Lady Bay.

Fletcher Jones Gardens, cnr Flaxman Street and Raglan Parade, are a colourful advocate for Victoria's claim as the Garden State of Australia. Thousands of visitors come each year to see these gardens.

The Performing Arts and Conference Centre, 185 Timor Street, is a modern-style building situated in landscaped grounds in the heart of the business and restaurant district.

Warrnambool

It has three main venues suitable for stage presentations, conventions, dinners, cabarets, exhibitions, lectures, classes and meetings. Check the daily newspapers for programmes, or ✆5564 7904.

Warrnambool Art Gallery, 165 Timor Street, has a permanent collection of 19th and 20th century Australian and European paintings and graphics - ⊙open daily noon-5pm, ✆5564 7832.

The **Warrnambool Botanic Gardens** are on the corner of Botanic and Queen Streets.

Tower Hill State Game Reserve, 14km (9 miles) from Warrnambool, is the remains of a volcano whose crater walls collapsed inward during its dying stages 6000 years ago. They blocked the 3km wide crater, which later filled with water. There is a sealed road leading to the main island, from where bushwalks radiate. There is also a **Natural History Centre**, ⊙open 9.00am to 4.30pm daily, which conducts tours, ✆5565 9202.

Hopkins Falls, are 13km (8 miles) from Warrnambool, near Wangoom. Thousands of tiny eels (elvers) make their way up the falls to the quiet waters beyond, to grow to maturity before returning to the sea to breed.

There are several recommended **heritage walks** through the town and nearby regions, and the Tourist Centre can provide you with maps and other details.

Warrnambool also has **a mystery**! There have been several reported sightings of the wreck of a mahogany ship in the windswept sandhills west of the city. The last was in 1980, and several artefacts have been found in the area. It is said that the ship foundered 400 years ago with a complement of Dutch and Spanish sailors. If there is any substance to the story it means that Europeans set foot on Australian soil long before Captain Cook. In 1980 the City Council formed a Mahogany Ship Committee to compile all the known information, which is being fed into a computer in an endeavour to solve the mystery.

Festivals

Wunta Fiesta - February.
Racing Carnival - May
Melbourne-Warrnambool Cycling Classic - October.

Facilities

Aerobics, badminton, basketball, volleyball, bingo, boating, lawn bowls, indoor cricket, croquet, golf, greyhound racing, horse racing, swimming, mini golf, scuba diving, skin diving, squash, speedway, surfing, swimming, table tennis, tennis, ten pin bowling, waterskiing, windsurfing and yachting.
Here are a few specific activity venues:
Karting
Indoor Karting, Silverton Park, ✆5562 2422. Open Wed-Fri noon-late, Sat-Sun 11am-late.
Golf
Mini Golf Lake Pertobe, 47 Pertrobe Road, ✆5562 0644. Open Dec-Jan - 10am-close, Feb-Nov - noon-5pm.
Horse-riding
Rundells Mahagany Trail Rides, Millers Lane, Dennington via Warrnambool, ✆5529 2303. One and two hour trail rides, full day pub rides, twilight rides and riding lessons. Horse riding mainly along the beach.
Fishing
Warrnambool Trout Farm, 4km north of Warrnambool on Wollaston Road, ✆019 94 3396. Catches guaranteed, equipment supplied free, fish feeding, barbecue. ⊙Open every weekend 10.30am-5pm, 7 days during school holidays.

Tours

Regular tours on the new **Sprit of Warrnambool**, lasting from 1-1.5 hours return. ⊙Open 10am-6pm with nighttime charters available. Adults ✪$10, children $5.
Southern Right Charters and Diving, ✆5561

6222 or ©5562 5044, offer fishing charters, diving charters, whale watching tours and scenic tours.

Seeall Tours, 13 Barham Avenue, ©5562 5795, have six tours through various locations, costing between ✪$10 and $50.

Warrnambool River Cruises, 2 Simpson Street, can be contacted on ©5562 7788.

Outlying Attractions

Great Ocean Road

The spectacular Great Ocean Road follows the coastline for much of its 250 kilometre (156 miles) length from Torquay to Peterborough. In some parts it is the only thing separating the mount-ains from the surf beaches.

The road was built by 3000 First World War veterans, and was ded-icated to the memory of all those who fought in that war. Using picks and shovels, the men commenced work in 1919 and the road was opened in 1932.

Fully sealed, though narrow in parts, it wends its scenic route through some of Victoria's most popular resorts. Pretty coastal towns like Lorne, Apollo Bay and Port Campbell swell to capacity in the high season. But it is in the winter, when massive breakers crash into the limestone cliffs, that the challenge which confronted the captains of the small coastal vessels can be understood. In the period to 1920, some 80 major shipping disasters were recorded between Port Fairy and Cape Otway. Of these the best known are the *Loch Ard* and the *Schomberg*, relics of which can be seen in the Flagstaff Hill Maritime Village at Warrnambool.

The road also passes through some of the richest forests in Australia. The Angahook Forest Park, the Otway National Park and the Lorne Forest Park are all extensive forest systems with prolific fauna.

We are starting our trip along the Great Ocean Road from Lorne, which is less than 2 hours' drive from Melbourne, and 218km (135

Warrnambool

miles) from Warrnambool.

As an additional resource, the website covering the general area is 🖰 www.greatoceanrd. org.au

Lorne

On the Erskine River, surrounded on three sides by forest ranges, and to the south by the Southern Ocean, Lorne was the first place declared an area of Special Significance and Natural Beauty by the Victorian Government.

On a bay named after Capt Louttit, who sought shelter there around 1840 while retrieving cargo from a shipwreck, Lorne was first settled by William Lindsay, a timber-cutter. Subdivision began in 1869 and the town was named after the Marquis of Lorne. Much of its colourful history is preserved in the gracious homes which remain.

Lorne's attractions include **Lorne Angahook State Park**, **Erskine Falls**, **Pennyroyal Valley**, as well as numerous bushwalks leading through lush fauna to beautiful waterfalls.

The Lorne Visitor Information Centre is at 144 Mountjoy Parade, ☏5289 1152. It is ⏰open daily 9am-5pm. They can provide you with excellent information on absolutely everything you need to know to about this area, from where to stay and eat, to what to see and do. If you wish to contact them by email, the address is ✉ lornevic@primus.com.au. The web page is 🖰www. surfcoast.vic.gov.au

Apollo Bay

Apollo Bay was first visited in 1840 by the Henty Brothers, founders of Portland and Mount Gambier. They established a small whaling station on what is now the golf course. One of the three major centres along the Great Ocean Road, it has all facilities to offer the visitor - motels, hotels, holiday flats, lodges and caravan parks; several restaurants and take-away food places.

There are also many guest houses, B&Bs and cottages in Apollo Bay, so if you prefer these cosy kinds of accommodation, the Information Centre can give you an idea of what is on offer. The Visitor Information Centre is on the Great Ocean Road, ☏(03) 5237 6529.

Apollo Bay is an ideal touring centre for the **Otway Ranges Forest Park**, **Otway National Park**, and **Melba Gully State Park**.

Princetown

Situated on the La Trobe Creek near Gellibrand River, the surrounding limestone cliffs contain interesting fossils and formations. Gemstones can sometimes be found along the coastline, and the area is rich in flora and fauna. Princetown was named after Prince Alfred and was proclaimed in 1885. Safe swimming, boating, fishing and water skiing are all features of this tiny settlement.

Given its location between the western boundary of the **Otway National Park** and the eastern boundary of the **Port Campbell National Park**, Princetown is ideal as a base for touring both.

Port Campbell

At the heart of one of Australia's most famed and photographed natural attractions, Port Campbell is a very popular resort. Situated on Campbell's Creek, and named after Capt. Alexander Campbell, a Scotsman in charge of the Port Fairy whaling station, it began as a small fishing port with surrounding pastoral runs. In 1964, 700ha (1729 acres) around Port Campbell was set aside as a National Park, and in 1981 the park was extended from Princetown through to Peterborough. Port Campbell is roughly at the centre of the park.

The town is a crayfishing port near the mouth of the river and has a safe, sandy beach ideal for family swimming. Restaurants and take-away foods are available and fresh local crayfish is the specialty.

Of course the **Port Campbell National Park** itself is the attraction (see entry opposite), but whilst in Port Campbell you can take a trip to the old cemetery on the northern edge

continued on page 102

Port Campbell National Park

Recognised as one of Australia's most scenic sections of coastline, the 1750ha (4323 acres) Port Campbell National Park stretches 32km (20 miles) along the Great Ocean Road.

The best known features are the **Twelve Apostles**, **Loch Ard Gorge** and **London Bridge**. In early 1990 a span of London Bridge collapsed into the ocean, vividly demonstrating the ongoing erosion of wind and sea on the limestone cliffs of the park.

Gorges, arches, islands, blowholes and stark outcrops create a dramatic foreground to the stormy Southern Ocean which stretches to the Antarctic. Here and there a sandy beach glistens in sharp contrast to the sheer cliffs and deep inlets which offer some of the most interesting scenery and photography subjects you will find.

Further information on the park can be acquired by calling   13 1963.

Warrnambool

Port Fairy

continued from page 100
of the town. It has many old graves of interest, including that of Captain Scott and some of his crew, shipwrecked off the coast in the barque *Newfield* in 1892.

A look-out on the western side of the river offers a scenic view of town and coastline.

The Port Campbell Visitor Information Centre, is in 26 Morris Street, ©5598 6089.

Peterborough
Situated at the mouth of the Curdie's River, Peterborough is a popular summer holiday town where you can get away from it all. River or beach swimming, and fishing for bream, mullet or crayfish are among the main pastimes, while the shipwrecks in the area provide good diving and aqualunging.

Port Fairy
The pretty town of Port Fairy is 29km (18 miles) from Warrnam-bool. The first stop for all visitors should be the Visitor Information Centre in 22 Bank Street, ©(03) 5568 2682, as this historic town has many attractions. Over 50 buildings have been classified by the National Trust, and there many art, craft and antique shops, picnic and barbecue areas, and facilities for golf, tennis, squash, lawn bowls and boat trips. There are heritage buildings outlined in brochures available from the Visitor Centre, and the Port Fairy History Centre in Gipps Street should satisfy anyone interested in nineteenth-century memorabilia.

High on the list of attractions, though, is not man-made. It is the **Mutton Bird Rookery** on Griffiths Island. The bird gets its name

from early settlers who utilised its fatty flesh for food, and as an oil source, but it is really the short-tailed shearwater (*puffinus tenuirostris*). They are not much to look at, but their lifestyle is fascinating. They arrive at Griffiths Island within three days of September 22 each year, returning to the nest burrow they had the previous year, with the same partner. They spend a few weeks renovating their homes, mate in early November, then fly out to sea for a couple of weeks. They return to Port Fairy about November 25, immediately lay their eggs (one per family), then both parents share in the incubation until the egg hatches in mid-January. After two or three days, the parents leave the chicks and forage at sea for food, firstly only for the day, regurgitating the food for the chicks at night, then gradually increasing the period and distance of food gathering until the chick has up to two weeks between meals. Nevertheless it gains weight rapidly and for a period becomes heavier than the adult birds. In mid-April the adult birds hear the call of the wild, commence their Pacific migration, and leave the young behind to fend for themselves. Hunger finally forces the chicks from the nest at night, and in early May they set off after the adults, somehow finding the migratory route with no help from mum or dad. Obviously, the mortality rate is high, and it is not helped by stray dogs and cats, and visitors who do not stick to the formed tracks, and tramp through the burrows instead. In fact, one year 80% of the young chicks were lost because some people were careless while exploring the area.

Warrnambool

Geelong

Population 145,300
Geelong is on the shores of Corio Bay, south-west of Melbourne.

Climate

Average temperatures: June max 25C (77F) - min 13C (55F); July max 14C (57F) - min 5C (41F).

Characteristics

Geelong is Victoria's premier regional city and, in fact, was a more important commercial cen-tre than Melbourne in the 1840s. It is the natural gateway to the richest wool and wheat areas of the world. The city has many antique and arts and crafts shops.

Cunningham Pier stretches out into the bay, and the foreshore has been revamped exten-sively to create a very pleasant aspect. The area features gardens, restaurants and more.

Visitor Information

The Geelong and Great Ocean Road Tourist Information Centre is in Stead Park on the Princes Highway, ☎(03) 5275 5797. More in-formation can be found at the Wool Museum on Mooraboool Street, ☎5222 2900 or ☎1800 620 888 (free call).

The website to visit is ☞www.greatoceanrd. org.au (there are no email contact facilities). The Melbourne website ☞www.melbourne. citysearch.com.au also lists information on Geelong.

If you are wandering around the city, keep in mind that there is an information outlet in the Market Square Shopping Centre in Moorabool Street. Another can be found on the corner of Princes Highway and St Georges Road, Corio.

Geelong

Accommodation

Following is a selection of hotels, with a guide to prices for a double room. The area code is 03.

Mercure Hotel Geelong, cnr Gheringhap & Myers Streets, ©5221 6844. 142 units, 3 suites, licensed restaurant, pool, spa, sauna - ✪$140.

Sundowner Chain Motor Inn, 13 The Esplanade, ©5222 3499. 35 units, licensed restaurant, sauna, pool - ✪$105-175.

Flag Inn Eastern Sands, 1 Bellerine Street, ©5221 5577. 25 units, restaurant, parking - ✪$95-125.

Rose Garden Motor Inn, 14 Settlement Road (Princes Highway), ©5241 9441. 15 units, spas, carport parking - ✪$85-115.

Aristocrat Waurnvale Motel, 90 Princes Highway, ©5241 8211. 14 units, spa bath, pool, playground - ✪$70-85.

Huntsman Innkeepers Motor Inn, 9 Aberdeen Street, ©5221 2177. 36 units, licensed restaurant (closed Sun), pool, spa, sauna - ✪$75-90.

Colonial Lodge Motel, 57 Fyans Street, ©5223 2266. 10 units - ✪$65-75.

The Ponds Hotel Motel, Princes Highway, ©5243 1244. 15 units, licensed restaurant - ✪$65-70.

Kangaroo Motel, 16 The Esplanade, ©5221 4022. 10 units, restaurant - ✪$70-75.

Caravan Parks

Barwon Caravan & Tourist Park, 153 Barrabool Road, ©5243 3842. (No pets allowed) 191 sites, barbecue, playground - powered sites ✪$20-25 for two, cabins $55-85 for two.

City Southside Caravan Park, 87 Barrabool Road, ©5243 3788. (No dogs allowed) 90 sites, barbecue, playground - powered sites ✪$18 for two, cabins $55-65 for two.

Billabong Caravan Park, 59 Barrabool Road, ©5243 6225. (No pets allowed) 97 sites, barbecue, playground, pool - powered sites ✪$18-20 for two, cabins $55-65 for two.

Sherwood Forest Caravan Park, 70 Bailey Street, ©5243 1068. (Pets allowed at owner's discretion) 120 sites, pool, playground - unpowered sites ✪$17 for two, cabins $40-45 for two.

Eating Out

Geelong has a good selection of restaurants, with all nationalities represented. Also, some of the motels have restaurants serving reasonably-priced meals. Recommended restaurants are:

Bamboleo, 86 Little Malop Street, ©5229 2548. Licensed restaurant with Spanish cuisine.

Rheingold Cellar, 9 Malop Street, ©5222 2557. Traditional German and Continental dishes. The restaurant has an historic theme and light entertainment to liven the atmosphere.

Le Parisien, 15 Eastern Beach Road, ©5229 3110. Licensed restaurant that has an extensive wine list boasting more than 350 selections. Waterside frontage and seafood specialities.

Empire Grill, 66 McKillop Street, ©5223 2132. Licensed, with regional wines, a-la-carte dining.

Mexican Graffiti, 43 Yarra Street, ©5222 2036. All types of Californian-style Mexican food available. Fully licensed. Open from 11am daily.

Mei Ling, 169 Malop Street, ©5229 7505. Chinese food with dine-in, take-away or home delivery options.

Fisherman's Pier, Bay end of Yarra Street, ©5222 4100. Fully licensed seafood restaurant overlooking Corio Bay. Outside dining, family oriented menu. Open daily for both lunch and dinner.

King Edward VII, above the Sailors Rest Tavern, 3 Moorabool Street, ©5224 2241. Modern international cuisine, alfresco dining, water views.

Pastels by the Bay, 13 The Esplanade, ©5222 3499. Fully licensed, bay views, open daily for lunch and dinner.

Pearl of China Cafe, 154 Ryrie Street, ©5229 8895. Take-away, home delivery or a-la-carte.

Sirinda, 93 Ryrie Street, ©5221 5797. Thai.

Koaki, Bell Parade, ©5272 1925. Traditional Japanese food.

Samraat, 137 Pakington Street, Geelong West, ©5229 7995. Indian cuisine.

McDonalds have branches on the corner of Ryrie and Yarra Streets, Geelong; 400 Melbourne Road, Geelong North; and 230-236 Autumn Street, Geelong West.

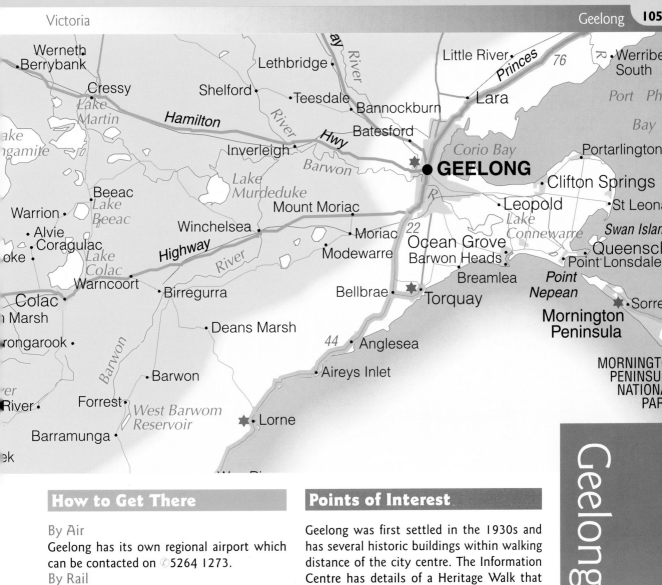

How to Get There

By Air
Geelong has its own regional airport which can be contacted on ☏5264 1273.

By Rail
Trains run frequently between Melbourne and Geelong, ☏13 1368.

By Coach
V/Line services Geelong frequently, ☏13 6196.

By Car
From Melbourne, via the Princes Highway (74km-46miles).

Points of Interest

Geelong was first settled in the 1930s and has several historic buildings within walking distance of the city centre. The Information Centre has details of a Heritage Walk that starts from the Post Office on the corner of Ryrie and Gheringhap Streets.

The National Wool Museum, cnr Moorabool & Brougham Streets, ☏5227 0701, is housed in a bluestone wool store and traces the story of wool from the sheep's back to the finished garment. Wool auctions are still held here. ⏱Open daily 9.30am-5pm, and admission is ✪$7 adults, $3.50 children and $18 for families.

Geelong Art Gallery, Little Mallop Street, ☏5229 3645, has some fine examples of early

Jan Juc Beach

Australian painters and a good contemporary collection. ⊙Open Mon- Fri 10am-5pm, Sat-Sun 1-5pm. Admission is free.

Port of Geelong Maritime Museum, Eastern Beach Road, ✆5277 2260, has displays depicting 150 years of shipping in Corio and Port Phillip Bays. The museum is ⊙closed on Tuesdays and Thursdays, and opens from 10am-4pm every other day of the week. Entry fees are ✪$2 adults, 50c children and $4 for families.

The Ford Discovery Centre, on the corner of Gheringap & Brougham Streets, ✆5227 8700, features the history of car design and engineering, and offers insights into the impact of global influences and environmental change on automobiles in the future. It is ⊙closed on Tuesdays but opens 10am-5pm every other day.

Gabbinbar Animal Wildlife Park, 654 Torquay Road, ✆5264 1455. Many types of animals, both native and foreign, can be found in the park ⊙open daily 10am-5pm.

Beaches. Apart from the still-water beaches in Corio Bay-Eastern Beach and St Helen's - there are the nearby still-water beaches of Port Phillip Bay - Portarlington, Indented Head, St Leonards, Queenscliffe and Barwon Heads. Then you come to the ocean beaches of Point Londsdale, Ocean Grove, Torquay, Jan Juc, Anglesea, Point Addis, Airey's Inlet, Fairhaven, Lorne, and the surfing mecca, Bell's Beach.

Festivals

The Springding Festival is held in November.

Facilities

There are facilities for over 150 sports, including football, basketball, horse racing, greyhound racing, golf, tennis, and all water sports.

Portland

Population 12,000
Portland is situated on the coast of Victoria at Cape Sir William Grant, and is the only deepwater port between Geelong and Adelaide.

Climate

Average temperatures: January max 22C (72F) - min 13C (55F); July max 12C (54F) - min 8C (46F). Average rainfall: 840mm (33 in); wettest 6 months May - October. Average hours of sunshine: summer 8; autumn 4; winter 3; spring 5.

Characteristics

Portland was the first permanent settlement in Victoria, and is filled with historic buildings from the 1840s. The Henty Brothers settled with their flocks of sheep in 1834 before Victoria was proclaimed a separate State.

Portland has become an important port serving a vast hinterland including the Mallee, Wimmera, Western District and the southeast of South Australia. It is also the site of the giant Portland Aluminium Smelter.

How to Get There

By Bus
There is a daily bus service to/from Mount Gambier which takes about 90 minutes.
By Rail
There is a rail service from Melbourne with a coach connection to Portland.
By Road
Either along the Princes Highway from Melbourne (362km - 225 miles), or via the Great Ocean Road from Melbourne.
Via the Princes Highway from Adelaide (568km - 353 miles), or the Calder and Henty Highways from Mildura (531km - 330 miles).

Portland

Accommodation

No shortage in this department in Portland. Here is a selection with prices for a double room per night, which should be used as a guide only. The telephone area code is 03.

Mariner Motel, 196 Percy Street, 5523 2877. 12 units - $55-70.

Admella Motel, 5 Otway Court, 5523 3347. 10 units, bbq - $57.

Whaler's Rest Motor Inn, 155 Henty Hwy, 5523 4077. 13 units, swimming pool, bbq - $80-105.

Melaleuca Motel, 25 Bentinck Street, 5523 3397. 16 units, unlicensed restaurant (closed Sunday) - $55.

Grosvenor Motel, 206 Hurd Street, 5523 2888. 14 units, unlicensed restaurant (Mon-Thurs), bbq - $65-85.

Caravan Parks

Centenary Caravan Park, 184 Bentinck Street, 5523 1487. (No dogs allowed) - powered sites $18 for two, cabins $18 for two.

Portland Haven Caravan Park, 76 Garden Street, 5523 1768. (No dogs allowed) - powered sites $14-16 for up to four, cabins $33-55 for up to four.

Henty Bay Caravan Park, Dutton Way, 5523 3716. (Dogs allowed under control) - powered sites $15-25 for two, on-site vans $25-40 for two.

Claremont Holiday Village, 37 Percy St, 5521 7567. (No dogs allowed) - powered sites $18-20 for two, cabins $40-72 for two.

Dutton Way Caravan Park, Dutton Way, 5523 1904. (Pets allowed at manager's discretion) - powered sites $13-16 for two, on-site vans $30-33 for two.

Eating Out

Here are a few reasonably priced eateries you might like to try:

The Canton Palace BYO Chinese Restaurant, 7 Julia Street, 5523 3677.

Middle Kingdom Chinese Restaurant, 31 Henty Street, 5523 3666.

Poon's Restaurant & Cafe, 121b Percy Street, 5523 5071.

Sandilands Restaurant, 33 Percy Street, 5523 3319.

Counter meals are available at *Richmond Henty Hotel*, 101 Bentinck Street, 5523 1032; *Mac's Hotel*, 41 Bentinck Street, 5523 2188; and *Gordon Hotel*, 63 Bentinck Street, 5523 1121.

Tourist Information

The Portland Maritime Discovery and Visitor Information Centre can be found in Lee Breakwater Road, (03) 5523 2671. They are open daily 9am-5pm.

Points of Interest

There are around 100 historically-important buildings in the city, many classified by the National Trust, and all giving parts of Portland an old world charm. Some buildings from the Henty era are the bluestone mansions 'Burswood' and 'Claremont' built in the 1850s, the Customs House and the Court House. There are five important old inns dating from 1842 and an Historical Museum is in one of them, the Caledonian Inn. The Portland Club and the Visitors Centre are from the same period.

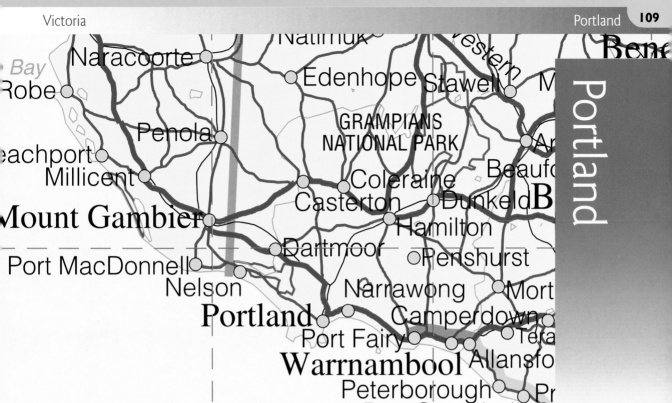

The Cottage in the Botanic Gardens, built in 1858, has been the home of six different curators over the years. It has now been restored and furnished in the period style of 120 years ago. The Cottage will be opened for inspection if you arrange an appointment, ✆5523 3820.

History House, the Old Town Hall, houses a collection of historical items, including the Henty plough. It contains, as well as large framed pictures of former mayors and prominent officials who were well known in the early days of the town, a fine collection of photographs and records of the early history of Portland. It ⊙open 10am-noon and 1-4pm every day, ✆5522 2226.

The 250km (155 miles) **Great South West Walk** provides an excellent introduction to the fascinating variety of scenery and wildlife in South-West Victoria. The walk begins and ends at the Visitor Centre and traverses forest, woodland, the Lower Glenelg National Park, the magnificent beaches at Discovery Bay, and the high limestone headlands at Cape Bridgewater and Cape Nelson. The walk is not solely for the hardy long distance walker, it can be undertaken in easy stages by young and old alike. A 2km section at Cape Grant has been sealed for the disabled.

Cape Bridgewater, is the home of the Petrified Forest, a tangle of weird tree forms fashioned by wind and water from the old root systems of the native scrub. The enormity of the rugged coastline can be experienced from cliff walks with the powerful ocean pounding the rocks below, and occasionally shooting up through blowholes.

Festivals

The Portland Summer Festival, Apex Fishing Carnival and Country and Music Festival are held in January. The Dahlia Festival is held in March.

Wannon Falls

Facilities

Boating, lawn bowls, bush walking, croquet, fishing, golf, horse riding, sailing, surfing, swimming, tennis, water skiing.

Outlying Attractions

Heywood

Situated 25km (16 miles) north of Portland, Heywood is a rural centre with hosts of apple orchards. The main attractions in the town are the Bower Bird Museum, ☏5527 1660, the Cave Hill Gardens, and Lake Condah Aboriginal Mission.

Hamilton

Known as the Wool Capital of the World, Hamilton is 58km (36 miles) north of Heywood in the heart of fine wool grazing country. The Tourist Information Centre is in Lonsdale Street, ☏5572 3746 or ☏1800 807 056 (free call), and they have information on the town's attractions, which include the Hamilton Art Gallery ☏5573 0460, Hamilton Historical Museum ☏5572 4933, the Pastoral Museum ☏5571 1595, Lake Hamilton and nearby Nigretta and Wannon Falls.

Macarthur

34km (21 miles) south of Hamilton, and 11km (7 miles) south of Byaduk Caves, Macarthur is also within easy reach of Mt Napier and its volcanic surrounds. Only a few kilometres south-west of the town is the Mt Eccles National Park, in which is found Lake Surprise. There are two first class walks around the crater of Mt Eccles, and camping and picnic facilities are available.

Nelson

Nelson is 70km (43 miles) west of Portland, and is a picturesque fishing hamlet at the mouth of the Glenelg River. It is a popular resort and has numerous bushwalks. A regular boat service takes visitors to the Margaret Rose Caves, which are ☉open daily for inspection, ☏8738 4191.

Victoria: An Overview

Australia is an island continent in the South Pacific Ocean. It is the smallest conti nent and the largest island in the world with a coastline of 19,650km. Its nearest neighbours are New Zealand and Papua New Guinea, while East Timor and Indonesia are a little further away, off the north-western coast.

The country has an area of 7,682,300 square kilometres and is divided into six states - New South Wales, Queensland, Victoria, Tasmania, South Australia and Western Australia - and two territories - Northern Territory and Australian Capital Territory.

The capital of Australia is Canberra in the Australian Capital Territory (ACT). The capital cities of the states are as follows:

New South Wales - Sydney
Victoria - Melbourne
Queensland - Brisbane
Tasmania - Hobart
South Australia - Adelaide
Western Australia - Perth
Northern Territory - Darwin.

History of Victoria

Settlers in Van Diemen's Land (Tasmania) had known for years that there was good grazing land in the Port Phillip area, but had been refused permission to settle there. In 1835, John Batman ignored the ban, landed with a party, and 'bought' 600,000 acres of land from the local Aborigines for a few axes and other trade goods. He then returned to Launceston and formed the Port Phillip Association. (On the north side of Flinders Street, between Market and William Streets, there is a small plaque in the pavement marking the place where Batman stood when he declared that it was a good place for a village.)

In 1836, Governor Bourke vetoed Batman's purchase, and appointed Captain William Lonsdale as resident magistrate of the rapidly-growing settlement.

Governor Burke visited the Port Phillip settlement in March 1837, and named the township 'Melbourne' after the Prime Minister of England. He approved the site and grid-plan of Melbourne, making minor changes to the plan of streets, naming them after important people, and began offering lots for sale.

The district experienced rapid growth, with the first government offices built in 1845, the first plantings in the Botanic Gardens in 1846 and the establishment of a mail service between Melbourne and Adelaide in 1847. Churches and Schools followed, the latter being established by both denominations.

Victoria officially became a separate colony on July 1st, 1851. Parliament house was commissioned, the site chosen in 1854, and construction begun in 1856. Also at this time, the growth of railways beginning in 1854, opened up the land beyond the Great Dividing Range. Wheat became Victoria's most valuable crop, surpassing even wool in importance.

The Australian Colonies Government Act was passed in August 1850, and constituted the Port Phillip district as a separate colony, with La Trobe as its first Lieutenant-Governor. Soon after, gold was discovered near Ballarat, and people came from all over the world seeking

Appendices

fortune. The consequent Eureka Uprising gave the new government its first major challenge.

Gold was first discovered in the Ballarat area in 1851 by James Esmond, and the rush for gold was on in earnest, with people coming from all over the world.

The government of the day had imposed a licence fee for the right to dig but didn't administer the system well, and there was the usual claim-jumping and skirmishes.

Tempers became short amongst the original miners, and the fields became a virtual tinder box. The Eureka uprising came about when a digger, James Scobie, was murdered, and a hotel owner named Bentley was charged with the crime, but found not guilty, contrary to popular belief. Led by Peter Lalor, about 120 men burnt thier licencse and built a stockade, flying their own flag, on the night of December 2, 1854. After a battle lasting barely twenty-five minutes, about 22 diggers and 6 soldiers were killed, and 114 prisoners were taken. The battle was lost, but the miners' rights improved as a consequence

In 1861, the first Melbourne Cup was held at the Victoria Turf Club at Flemington. The town was excited by this large event and even the news fo the Burke and Wills Failed expedition to he Gulf of Carpentaria could not dampen the festive atmosphere, and the annual November event was born.

Over the next 40 years, Victoria grew in industry and influence, despite Economic Depression and Industrial strikes in the late 1890s, as Australia moved towards Federation. In March 1901, the new Commonwealth of Australia was established and Melbourne was chosen as the home of the Parliament until a permanent location for the new capital city was chosen (eventually Canberra in 1927). Edmund Barton became the first Prime Minister of Australia.

The following 30 years saw change to the state as women gained the right to vote in 1908, and the introduction of the motor car changed approaches to industry and travel.

While the onset of the First World War resulted in huge price hikes for metropolitan Victorians, country people by contrast enjoyed a period of stability for their industries. This was due to the Commonwealth controlling markets for wool, meat and dairy also brought great benefits to rural communities. In contrast, the gold industry slumped to near extinction throughout the war years.

The 1930s were a difficult time with widespread unemployment, the depression, and the Black Friday bushfires of 1939. After the Second World War, Victoria enjoyed more stability, until the political 'split' of the Australian Labour Party, in 1955, partly the result of anti-Communist hysteria. The formation of the new Democratic Labour Party, saw the beginning of 27 years of conservative government in Victoria.

In 1956, the world's attention centred on Victoria as it hosted the Summer Olympic Games. This was also the year of Australia's first television broadcasts. The next few decades were politically turbulent, with the constitutional crisis of 1975, in which Gough Whitlam's Federal Labour government was dismissed by Australia's Governor General, and Labour's return from Victorian political exile in 1982.

Joan Kirner became Victoria's first female Premier on 10th August 1990, remaining in the position until the defeat of the Labour government in the 1992 general election. The next seven years of Liberal government under Jeff Kennet saw large reductions in public expenditure on education and health, the amalgamation of local councils and privatisation of public utilities. During this time the Australian Grand Prix was moved to Melbourne as an annual event, and the $2.3 billion Crown Casino was constructed.

The Labour party returned to power in 1999, and remains in office at the time of printing. Today, the state of Victoria is a vibrant and passionate state, leading Australia in many areas and recognised for its cultural diversity.

Australian Population

During the 1950s and 1960s, people wishing to migrate from Europe and the United States were provided with assisted passage by the Australian government. However, it was not until the late 1960s that restricted entry to Australia from Asia was eased. In the last 40 years Australian society has undergone a tremendous change with now one in four people being a migrant or the child of a migrant.

Australia since the 1970s has become aware of its presence in South-east Asia. The countries of the region are starting to have more of an impact on Australian life. Many new migrants are Asian, and society reflects this blend of European and Asian cultures.

Approximately 85 per cent of the 18,783,600 inhabitants live in urban areas. The east coast of Australia is the most populous because of the fertile plain east of the Great Dividing Range of mountains. The major cities are the state capitals, and the most populous state is New South Wales with 6,173,000 people, followed by Victoria with 4,533,300 people.

The social environment is heavily influenced by the US media and movies. California has a lot in common with Australia's east coast.

Australian Holidays

Christmas, New Year and Anzac Day (April 25) are the only holidays that are held at the same time throughout the country. Easter is a moveable feast that can fall in either March or April. Australia Day is accepted by all as January 26, but some states have their public holiday on the exact day, and others choose the closest Monday, granting a long weekend.

The whole of Australia stops for five minutes on the first Tuesday in November for the running of the Melbourne Cup horse race, but only Melbourne residents have the day off.

In addition, school holidays are different in each state, although the long Christmas break is the most popular holiday time, and runs roughly from the end of the second week in December to the end of January.

It is a good idea to check with the Visitor Information Centres in the cities and towns before or upon arrival, as prices and availability of services are affected on public holidays.

Australian Language

Australians speak English, although due to the many people from other countries that have come to live in the country, it is not unusual to hear conversations in other languages when travelling by public transport. Melbourne, for instance, has the second largest Greek population of any city in the world, surpassed only by Athens.

Like the English, Australians call 'gas' petrol and 'fries' chips; but you will find links to the US are perhaps stronger, with McDonalds, Pizza Hut and KFC firmly established in every suburb. There are a few words and phrases that are unique to Australia and in common usage, and dictionaries of Australian slang are available at local bookshops. Australians do say "G'Day", and if stressing authenticity or the truth of a statement, they might say that something is "fair dinkum" or "dinky-di".

Australian Religion

The vast majority of Australians belong to the Christian Churches. There is only a slight margin between Roman Catholics and Anglicans, whose numbers hover around 26% each, reflecting the influence of migrating Irish and Italian Catholics, and the steady flow of English Anglicans into the country. All other religions and sects are present in Australia. Jews, Hindus and Buddhists are all represented strongly on account of the post World War II influx and other political developments since, which opened access to Australian shores. By and large there is peaceful coexistence, and the multicultural composition of society is typically celebrated and embraced.

Appendices

Australia: General Info

Entry Regulations

All travellers to Australia need a valid passport, and visitors of all nationalities, except New Zealand, must obtain a visa before arrival. These are available at Australian Embassies, High Commissions and Consular offices listed in local telephone directories. No vaccinations are required.

Before you land you will be given immigration forms as well as Customs and Agriculture declarations. As a general rule you must declare all goods of plant or animal origin. Quarantine officers will inspect these items and return them to you if no disease or pest risk is involved. Even if they are not prohibited, some may need to be treated before being allowed entry.

Each incoming traveller over the age of 18 years is allowed duty free goods to the value of $400, plus 1125mL of liquor and 250g of tobacco products. These items must not be intended for commercial purposes and you must carry them with you through customs.

Exit Regulations

There is a Passenger Movement Charge or Departure Tax of $30 for everyone over the age of 12 years, but this is generally prepaid with inclusion in the price of an airline ticket. People taking money out of the country, above the value of A$10,000 in Australian and/or foreign currency, must file a report with Customs. For more information on Customs or Quarantine Regulations, visit the following web sites:

👁 www.aqis.gov.au for Quarantine
👁 www.customs.gov.au for Customs

GST Refund

Overseas visitors qualify for a part refund of any GST they pay for items bought in Australia, if the total purchases made at any one business exceeds $300, and the purchases were made no more than 30 days before the date of departure. Present the goods, a tax invoice, your passport and a boarding pass at the TRS (Tax Refund Scheme) booth in the international airport you are leaving from. The items on which you are allowed to claim back GST are only the hand-held items you intend to carry with you onto the plane. Present your documents for verification and you will be given the refund to which you are entitled. If the total is less than $200 you can ask for the refund to be made in cash, otherwise it will be in the form of a mailed cheque or a credit arrangement. Foreign currency will also be accommodated in this transaction. Note that any general consumption purchases made within Australia (for example, hotel accommodation or meals) do not qualify for a refund claim.

Be aware that there is no GST imposed on duty-free items sold in duty-free stores.

For further details and enquiries, phone the Australian Customs Information Line on ✆ 1300 363 263.

Embassies

Nearly seventy countries have diplomatic representation in Canberra. Some missions are called Embassies, and others who represent countries belonging to the Commonwealth, are called High Commissions. There are also Consuls in the State capitals, and their addresses can be found in the local White Pages telephone directory.

Money

The Australian Currency is decimal, with the dollar as the basic unit. Notes come in a colourful array of $100, $50, $20, $10 and $5 denominations, with minted coins for lesser amounts - gold $1 and $2 coins, and silver 50c, 20c, 10c and 5c.

Currency exchange facilities are available at international airports, and most banks and large hotels.

The Australian dollar tends to fluctuate quite frequently. For the most accurate and up-to-date currency conversions, it is recommended that you use the simple and easy facility at ☞www. xe.com/ucc

Travellers cheques are one of the most convenient ways of carrying money when travelling, and these can be exchanged at any bank, large hotels, and in large department stores.

Automatic Teller Machines are another possibility. These machines are widely available in Australia, both in the cities and in country towns, and most are open 24 hours a day. Some banks allow access to overseas savings accounts via networks such as Cirrus and Plus, but it's best to check with your bank before departure to see if this is available.

If you are intending to stay for any great length of time, you might consider opening a local bank account. Different banks have different withdrawal limits, but it is generally about $1000 per day. All Australian banks operate this type of account.

Eating Out

In every town and city in this guide we have included a selection of restaurants, and have stated whether they are licensed or unlicensed (BYO). Just to confuse everyone, some restaurants are both, so if you are unsure, check when reserving your table. Without going into the licensing laws of why this is so, here is a short explanation of how it will affect patrons.

A licensed restaurant has a wine list, and can provide beer, mixed drinks, ports, liqueurs, etc. Patrons are not allowed to provide their own drinks.

A BYO restaurant does not have a licence, so you Bring Your Own wine or beer or whatever. Glasses are provided, and a corkage fee (for opening the bottles!) may be charged, which is usually around $1.50 per bottle. The restaurant usually has a selection of soft drinks, mineral water and fruit juices.

A restaurant that is licensed and BYO can provide alcohol, but you have the choice of bringing your own wine (which is often cheaper), but you are not allowed to bring your own beer or mixed drinks.

Liquor stores in Australia are called 'bottle shops'. Many hotels have one, usually with its own street entrance, and there's one in every shopping centre.

Miscellaneous

Telephones

If you are calling any Australian number from overseas, dial 61 for the country code and then a single number for the area code (for example, when calling Sydney, in New South Wales, you would dial 2), then the eight digit number. Area codes refer to states rather than districts. If calling from interstate, use the following prefix before any number you dial to: New South Wales- (02), Australian Capital Territory- (02), Victoria- (03), Tasmania- (03), Queensland- (07), South Australia- (08), Western Australia- (08), Northern Territory- (08)

Public telephones are easy to find in the cities and suburbs on street corners, in hotels, shops, cafes, and so on. A local call costs 40c from a phone box, but may be dearer from the privately leased phones outside shops. Emergency calls are free.

For international calls, you can dial direct to nearly 20 countries from almost any hotel, home, office or public phone in Australia. Simply dial 0011 + country code + area code + local number. Country Direct is the easiest

Appendices

Appendices

way of making international telephone card and reverse charge (collect) calls. Upon dialling your Country Direct number, you are immediately put in touch with your own country's operator who will then connect the call. To find out your country's number ℂ1800 801 800 (free call).

Newspapers

Morning and afternoon newspapers are available everywhere, with each state having their own press, as well as selling the national paper *The Australian*.

Radio and Television

There is a national radio station and a national television channel, both of which are run by the Australian Broadcasting Commission (ABC). The capital cities have many AM and FM radio stations, and several free-to-air television channels. The television channels are: 2 (the national channel), 7 (commercial), 9 (commercial), 10 (commercial) and 0 (SBS, which is government sponsored.

Post

Australia has an efficient postal service, and postcards sent by airmail to overseas countries cost $1. To send a letter by Air Mail (weighing up to 50g) to the Asia Pacific Zone costs $1 and to the Rest of the World, $1.50.

Time Zones

Australia is divided into three time zones: **Australian Eastern Standard Time, which covers Queensland, NSW, Victoria and Tasmania, is GMT plus 10 hours;** Australian Central Standard Time, which covers South Australia and the Northern Territory, is GMT plus 9.5 hours; and Australian Western Standard Time, which covers Western Australia, is GMT plus 8 hours.

During summer, some of the states operate on daylight saving putting their clocks ahead one hour on a designated Sunday morning in October, and back one hour on a Sunday in March. For NSW, Victoria and South Australia, it is the last Sunday in October and the first Sunday in March, but Tasmania remains on Summer Time until the end of March. West-

ern Australia, Queensland and the Northern Territory do not have daylight saving, so at those times there are five different time zones in the country.

Credit Cards

American Express, Diners Club, Visa, Bank Card and MasterCard are widely accepted and usually signposted at participating retail outlets.

Beaches

Australian beaches are famous throughout the world, and they certainly live up to their reputation. All have white sandy shores, and rolling surf. Some offer better waves than others, and the bigger beaches are usually divided into sections for swimmers and for board riders.

The Surf Lifesaving Clubs which patrol the beaches during summer are often staffed by voluntary workers, young people who give up their weekends and holidays to keep a watchful eye out for others. They put up flags to show which part of the beach is safest for swimmers, and there are usually signs requesting people to swim between the flags. This is good advice - don't ignore it.

Electricity

Domestic electricity supply throughout Australia is 230-250 volts, AC 50 cycles. Standard three pin plugs are fitted to domestic appliances. 110v appliances, such as hairdryers and contact lens sterilisers, cannot be used without a transformer.

Videos

Australia uses the PAL system of videos. For the US market, tapes must be the NTSC system.

Internet General Information Sources

For general information on Australia, the best site to explore is
👁www.australia.com,
which is the official web page of the Australian Tourist Commission.

For phone numbers nationwide, go to:
👁www.whitepages.com.au
👁www.yellowpages.com.au
👁www.colourpages.com.au

Travel Information

How To Get to Victoria

To reach Victoria and Australia from overseas, visitors must come either by air or sea.

Before booking a flight, it is best to shop around for any cheaper fares that may be available. Your travel agent will be able to advise. You may also be able to find a Package Tour that meets all your requirements. These save you money because the companies that organise them can obtain cheaper fares and accommodation prices, as they are booking for groups. Again, your travel agent is the best person to ask.

Accommodation

Australia has well-developed hotel and motel accommodation in cities, resorts and rural areas. A typical room is usually spotlessly clean and has air-conditioning, a private bathroom, tea and coffee making facilities, a telephone, television, and a small refrigerator. Note that some small hotels may not have a private bathroom for every room, and it is best to enquire when booking. Because of the climate, many hotels and motels have small outdoor swimming pools.

Although the rooms are often the same, there is a difference between a hotel and a motel in Australia. A hotel must have a public bar among its facilities; motels often provide a bar for paying guests and invited friends, although they are not obliged to do this. Most hotels and motels have a dining room or restaurant.

Premier class hotels include names familiar throughout the world - Hilton, Sheraton, Hyatt, Nikko, Holiday Inn, Intercontinental, Marriott, Ibis and Mercure, can all be found in Australia's major cities.

Motels have generally been developed to meet the needs of travelling motorists and are located in cities, towns and resorts, and along the major highways.

The majority of hotels and motels offer accommodation on a room-only basis, but some include one or more meals in their tariff. Enquire about any meals that might be automatically included in the room price and check whether you can pay just for the room, if this suits your travel schedule better. For example, there is no point paying for lunch if you plan on leaving before daybreak, or for a dinner if you know you won't reach your destination until late.

Youth Hostels in most parts of the country offer an inexpensive alternative for budget conscious travellers. Membership of the Youth Hostels Association is required, ✆ 9261 1111. They have a comprehensive internet site showing all the hostel locations at 👁 www.yha.com.au or you can send an email to the address: ✉ yha@yhansw.org.au

Most towns and holiday resorts have caravan parks and camping grounds with shower and toilet facilities, at very reasonable rates. Caravan parks usually have some cabins or on-site vans available for overnight or longer stays. This is a comparatively inexpensive form

Appendices

of accommodation, but it usually means that you have to have your own bed linen, blankets and pillows.

Travelling Within Australia

By Air

The major interstate carrier is Qantas, ✆13 1313. Virgin Blue, ✆13 6789 also offers limited services. Both offer reduced fares and 'specials' from time to time, and it is best to find out what is available when you intend to travel.

At the time of printing, the airlines listed above are in the process of significant changes, so it is best to check with an AFTA travel agent, listed in the phone book, about regional flights at the time of your trip.

By Rail

Train travel is possible between Sydney, Brisbane and Melbourne. Most towns in between are also linked, as well as those in popular outlying areas of each state. Rail Australia offers two rail passes that can only be purchased outside of Australia:

Austrail Flexipass - 8 (✪$550), 15 (✪$800), 22 (✪$110) or 29 (✪$1440) days travel in 6 months with unlimited stopovers, in economy class.

Austrail Pass - unlimited travel for 14 (✪$660), 21 (✪$860) or 30 (✪$1035) days consecutively anywhere in Australia, including metropolitan services, in economy class.

Passes that are available within Australia include:

East Coast Discovery Pass - travel one-way with unlimited stopovers in a six month period: Brisbane to Cairns (✪$160); Sydney to Brisbane/Gold Coast (✪$94); Sydney to Cairns (✪$248); Melbourne to Brisbane/Gold Coast (✪$176); Melbourne to Cairns (✪$228). Note that the above rates apply to travel in the opposite direction.

Countrylink Discovery Pass - unlimited use of Countrylink trains and connecting coaches for 14 (✪$165), 30 (✪$198), 90 (✪$220), or 180 (✪$330) days.

Queensland Road Rail Pass - unlimited use of Queensland Rail services (long-distance) and McCaffertys Coaches for any 10 days over a 60 day period (✪$286) or any 20 days over a 90 day period (✪$374).

To get the latest prices, visit the Rail Australia web site at ☞www.railaustralia.com.au/pass_rates.htm

By Bus

The major interstate coach companies are Greyhound Pioneer and McCafferty's. Tickets for both companies are now interchangeable.

McCafferty's can be contacted on ✆13 1499, or ☞www.mcaffertys.com.au

Aussie Passes: a pre-selected travel route along which you can stop off at designated points.

All Australian
Validity: 365 days, Cost: ✪$2100 full fare, ✪$1790 concession.

Aussie Highlights
Route: Melbourne - Sydney - Brisbane - Cairns - Uluru (Ayers Rock) - Adelaide - Canberra and many other outback, rural and coastal destinations in between.
Validity: 365 days, Cost: ✪$1255 full fare, ✪$1066 concession.

Sunseeker
Validity: 183 days, Cost: ✪$411 full fare, ✪$349 concession.

Best of the East
Validity: 365 days, Cost: ✪$1026 full fare, ✪$872 concession.

Coast to Coast
Validity: 183 days, Cost: ✪$424 full fare, ✪$360 concession.

Reef & Rock
Validity: 183 days, Cost: ✪$596 full fare, ✪$507 concession.

Outback & Reef
Validity: 183 days, Cost: ✪$726 full fare, ✪$617 concession.

An Aussie Kilometre Pass, valid for 12 months, allows you to 'bulk buy' the distance you think you will need to cover for your holiday, at a rate designed to increase your value for money with every kilometre purchased. Prices range from ✪$281 for 2000km to ✪$1077 for 10,000km to ✪$1975 for 20,000km.

By Road

Australians drive on the left-hand side of the road, and the speed limit in built-up areas is 50km/h or 60km/h, and on the open road up to 110km/h.

In an effort to cut the number of road fatalities, Australia has random breath testing which is carried out by police officers either from a standard police car or from what are known locally as 'booze buses'. The allowable blood alcohol level varies from state to state, but is generally around 0.05, or two standard drinks in the first hour and only one during every subsequent hour. But since body tolerance levels differ, it is best simply not to drink if you expect to drive soon after.

To get to individual areas of Victoria, see the *How to Get There* section at the beginning of each chapter in this book

Travelling to and around Victoria
By Air
As Mentioned Above, the major interstate carrier is Qantas, 13 13 13. Virgin Blue, 13 6789 also offers services to Victoria. Flight times and prices vary throughout the year, so it is best to examine them ahead of time.
By Rail
To get to Melbourne, there are rail services from Sydney and Adelaide, with connections from other capital cities, ✆13 2232. The country and interstate terminal in Melbourne is Spencer Street Station.
V/Line
Rail and coach services operate from country Victoria to Melbourne daily. They also travel as far as Adelaide, Canberra and the Sapphire Coast of NSW. For further information, ✆136196.
By Road
To get to Melbourne from Sydney, via the Hume Highway, 875km (544 miles); via the Princes Highway, 1058km (657 miles); via the Olympic Way, 961km (597 miles); via Canberra/Cooma/Cann River, 1038km (645 miles).

From Adelaide, via the Western and Dukes Highways, 726km (451 miles); via Princes Highway West, 910km (565 miles).

Appendices

General Index

A

ABC 116
Accommodation 117
Acknowledgements 6
Air Mail 116
Airey's Inlet 106
alcohol blood level 119
Alexandra 48
Alexandra Fountain 66
Alexandra Gardens 85
American Express 116
Anglesea 106
Apollo Bay 100
Ararat 83
Ararat & The Grampians 83
  Accommodation 84
  Characteristics 83
  Eating Out 84
  Facilities 85
  Festivals 85
  How to Get There 83
  Outlying Attractions 85
  Points of Interest 85
Ararat Art Gallery 85
Ararat Town Hall 85
Arch of Victory 80
Area codes 115
Arthur's Seat Scenic Chairlift 35
Ashcombe Maze 35
Aussie Kilometre Pass 119
Aussie Passes 118

Australia: General Info 114
  Eating Out 115
  Embassies 114
  Entry Regulations 114
  Exit Regulations 114
  GST Refund 114
  Miscellaneous 115
  Money 115
Australian Eastern Standard Time 116
Australian Broadcasting Commission 116
Australian Central Standard Time 116
Australian Dairy Centre 35
Australian Gallery of Sport & Olympic Museum 27
Australian Holidays 113
Australian Language 113
Australian Motorcycle Grand Prix 33
Australian Population 113
Australian Religion 113
Australian Rules Football 33
Australian Tennis Open 33
Australian, The, Newspaper 116
Australian Western Standard Time 116
Automatic Teller Machines 115
Avenue of Honour 80
Avoca 82

Index

B

Badger Weir 46
Bairnsdale 44
Ballarat 75
    Accommodation 76
    Characteristics 75
    Eating Out 77
    Facilities 81
    Festivals 81
    How to Get There 75
    Outlying Attractions 81
    Points of Interest 77
    Tourist Information 76
Ballarat Fine Art Gallery 78
Ballarat Tramway Museum 80
Ballarat Wildlife Park 78
Bank Card 116
Barmah Forest 74
Barwon Heads 106
Bass 35
Beaches 116
Beaches around Geelong 106
Bell's Beach 106
Benalla 61
Bendigo 63
    Accommodation 64
    Characteristics 63
    Climate 63
    Eating Out 64
    Facilites 68
    Festivals 68
    How to Get There 63
    Outlying Attractions 68
    Points of Interest 65
    Tourist Information 64
Bendigo Heritage Walk 65
Bendigo Market Place 67
Bendigo Pottery 67
Bicycle Hire 15
Blood on the Southern Cross 78
Botanical Gardens 80
bottle shops 115

Bright 49
Bright & the Victorian Alps 49
    Accommodation 50
    Characteristics 49
    Eating Out 51
    Festivals 52
    How to Get There 49
    Outlying Attractions 52
    Points of Interest 51
    Tourist Information 50
Bright Art Gallery & Cultural Centre 51
Bright Autumn Festival 52
Budget Forms 128
Buchan 42
Bus ticket prices 118
BYO 115
BYO restaurant 115

C

Cape Bridgewater 109
Cape Conran 42
Capitol Theatre 28
Car Hire 15
Castlemaine 68
Central Business District of Ballarat 78
Chinatown 26
Chinese Joss House 66
Chinese Museum 26
Churchill Island 34
City Explorer Bus 22
City Tour, Melbourne 31
Citylink 15
Clunes 81
coach companies 118
Coal Creek Heritage Village 35
Collins Street 20
Como House 29
Contents 5
Cooks' Cottage 27
Cottage in the Botanic Gardens 109
Credit Cards 116
Cricket Ground, Melbourne. *See* Melbourne
    Cricket Ground

Index

Croajinolong National Park 42
Crown Casino 28
Crown Entertainment Complex 28
currency conversions 115
Customs 114

D

Dandenong Ranges 36
Daylesford 82
daylight saving 116
Diners Club 116
Dinosaur World Fun Park & Fossil Museum 81
Discovery & Science Technology Centre 67
Dolls on the Avenue 92
Donnelly's Weir 46
Dookie College of Agriculture and Horticulture
     60
Driver Education Centre of Australia 60
driving in Australia 119
driving in Melbourne 15
Driving Tours from Ararat 85

E

Eagle Point 44
Eaglehawk 67
Eastbank Centre 59
Eating Out 115
Echuca 69
Echuca-Moama 69
   Accommodation 70
   Characteristics 69
   Climate 69
   Eating Out 70
   Facilities 73
   Festivals 73
   How to Get There 69
   Outlying Attractions 74
   Points of Interest 71
   Tourist Information 71

Edith Cavell Memorial 85
Eildon 48
Electricity 116
Embassies 114
Entry Regulations 114
Erskine Falls 100
Esplanade, The 29
Espsom Market 67
Eureka Memorial and Park 78
Eureka Museum 78
Eureka Stockade Centre 78
Euroa 62
Exit Regulations 114

F

Fairhaven 106
Falls Creek 54
Federation Square 27
Fire Services Museum Victoria 26
Fitzroy Gardens 27
Flagstaff Hill Maritime Museum 97
Flemington Racecourse 30
Fletcher Jones Gardens, 97
Floral Clock 27
Ford Discovery Centre 106
Formula One Grand Prix 33
French Island National Park 35

G

Gabbinbar Animal Wildlife Park 106
Gallery 90 51
Gaol, Old Melbourne 23
Geelong 103
   Accommodation 104
   Characteristics 103
   Climate 103
   Eating Out 104
   Facilities 106
   Festivals 106
   How to Get There 105
   Points of Interest 105
   Visitor Information 103

Index

Geelong Art Gallery 105
Geelong Maritime Museum 106
George Adams Gallery 28
Getting to Australia 117
Giant Worm Museum 35
Gippsland 43
Gold Museum 78
Golden Dragon Museum and Chinese Gardens 66
Golden River Zoo 92
Goldfields history 77
Goods and Services Tax 7
Grainger Museum 30
Grampians National Park 87
Grampians, The 83
Great Ocean Road 99
Great South West Walk 109
Great Western 87
Green Hill Lake 85
Greyhound Pioneer 118
Greyhound Pioneer/McCaffertys 10
greyhound racing 33
Griffiths' Sea Shell Museum and Marine Display 40
GST 114
GST Refund 114
Gumbuya Recreation and Leisure Park 35

H

Halls Gap 88
Hamilton 110
Hargreaves Mall 67
Hattah-Hulkyne National Park 94
Healesville 45
Healesville & The Yarra Valley 45
   Accommodation 46
   Characteristics 45
   Climate 45
   Eating Out 46
   Facilities 48
   Festivals 48
   Outlying Attractions 48
   Points of Interest 46
   Tourist Information 45

Healesville Sanctuary 46
Hedgend Maze 46
Hellenic Antiquities Museum 23
Hepburn Springs 81
Heywood 110
Historic Montrose Cottage 78
Historical Museum 59
Historical Museum of Bright 51
Historical Society Museum 71
History House, Portland 109
History of Victoria 111
Holidays 113
Hopkins Falls 98
How To Get to Australia 117
How to Use This Book 7
   Accommodation and Eating Out 7
   Goods and Services Tax 7
   Layout 7
   Symbols 7

I

IMAX Theatre 22
Immigration Museum 22
Indented Head 106
international phone calls 115
Internet General Information Sources 116

J

Jan Juc 106

K

Kennington Reservoir 67
Kings Domain 27
Kinkuna Country Fun Park & Zoo 40
Koala Conservation Centre 34
Kryal Castle 81
Kyabram 74

Index

Index

L

La Trobe's Cottage 27
Lake Condah Aboriginal Mission 110
Lake Pertobe Park 97
Lake Weeroona 67
Lake Wendouree 80
Lakes Entrance 37
  Accommodation 39
  Characteristics 37
  Climate 37
  Eating Out 40
  Facilities 42
  Festivals 39
  How to Get There 37
  Outlying Attractions 42
  Points of Interest 40
  Visitor Information 38
Lakes Entrance Aboriginal Art & Crafts 40
Langi Morgala Museum 85
Language 113
Library, State 23
limestone caves 42
Liquor stores 115
Loch Ard Gorge 101
London Bridge 101
Lorne 100, 106
Lorne Angahook State Park 100
Luna Park 29

M

Macarthur 110
Mail 116
Mallacoota 42
Mansfield 61
Maps Index 132
Maroondah Reservoir 46
Maryborough 82
Marysville 48
MasterCard 116
Maude Street Mall 59
McCafferty's 118
Melba Gully State Park 100

Melbourne 9
  Accommodation 11
  Climate 9
  Eating Out 16
  Entertainment 19
  Festivals 32
  How to Get There 10
  Local Transport 14
  Outlying Attractions 34
  Points of Interest 22
  Shopping 20
  Sporting Facilities 32
  Tours 31
  Visitor Information 10
Melbourne Aquarium 28
Melbourne Cricket Ground 27, 33
Melbourne Cup 32
Melbourne Discovery Pass 31
Melbourne Exhibition and Events Centre 28
Melbourne International Airport 10
Melbourne Museum 22
Melbourne Town Hall 28
Melbourne Zoo 30
Met, The 14
Mildura 89
  Accommodation 90
  Characteristics 89
  Climate 89
  Eating Out 91
  Facilities 92
  How to Get There 89
  Outlying Attractions 92
  Points of Interest 91
  Tourist Information 90
Moama 69
Money 115
Montrose Cottage 78
Moomba Festival 32
Mornington Peninsula 35
Mount Buffalo 53
Mount Buller 60
Mount Cole Forest 85
Mount Hotham 55
Mt Buffalo. *See* Mount Buffalo

Mungo National Park 94
Murray River Aquarium 72
Murray-Kulkyne National Park 94
Mutton Bird Rookery 102
Myer Music Bowl 27
Myrtleford 56

N

Nagambie 62
National Trust (Victoria) 32
National Wool Museum 105
Natural History Centre 98
Nelson 110
Newspapers 116
Ninety Mile Beach 40
Njernda 72
Nowa Nowa 42
Numurkah 60
Nyerimilang Park 40

O

Ocean Grove 106
Old Melbourne Gaol 23
Old Treasury 26
Omeo 42
One Tree Hill Lookout 67
Orange World 92
Orbost 42
Otway National Park 100
Otway Ranges Forest Park 100

P

PAL system of videos 116
Pall Mall 65
Parkville 30
Parliament House 26
Paynesville 44
Penguin Parade Visitors Centre 34
Peninsula Princess 35
Pennyroyal Valley 100

Performing Arts and Conference Centre 97
Performing Arts Museum 28
Peterborough 102
Phillip Island 34
phone calls 115
Photo Log 131
Point Addis 106
Point Londsdale 106
Polly Woodside Maritime Museum 28
Population, Australian 113
Porepunkah 52
Port Campbell National Park 100, 101
Port Fairy 102
Port of Echuca 71
Port of Geelong Maritime Museum 106
Portarlington 106
Portland 107
   Accommodation 108
   Characteristics 107
   Climate 107
   Eating Out 108
   Facilities 110
   How to Get There 107
   Outlying Attractions 110
   Points of Interest 108
   Tourist Information 108
Post 116
postal service 116
Princes Bridge 28
Princes Bridge Hotel 28
Princetown 100
Public telephones 115
Pyrenees House 85

Q

QANTAS 118
Quarantine 114
Queen Victoria Gardens 27
Queen's Park 46
Queenscliffe 106

Index

Index

R

racing, greyhound 33
Radio and Television 116
Radio Australia 60
Rail Australia 118
Rail pass prices 118
random breath testing 119
Red Cliffs 92
Regulations, Entry and Exit 114
Religion 113
Rialto Towers 23
Rippon Lea 29
Ripponlea Railway Station 30
River Cruises 92
Rochester 74
Royal Botanic Gardens 28
Royal Exhibition Building 22

S

Sale 44
Scienceworks Museum 23
Seal Rocks Life Centre 35
Seymour 62
Sharps Magic Movie House and Penny Arcade 72
Shepparton 57
  Accommodation 58
  Characteristics 57
  Climate 57
  Eating Out 58
  Facilities 60
  Festivals 60
  How to Get There 57, 58
  Outlying Attractions 60
  Points of Interest 59
  Visitor Information 59
Shepparton Art Gallery 59
Shepparton Preserving Company 60
Shepparton Sports Stadium 60
Shrine of Remembrance 27
Snow Country 53

Snowy River 42
Soccer 33
Sovereign Hill 79
Sprit of Warrnambool 98
St Kilda 29
St Leonards 106
St Patrick's Cathedral 26
St Paul's Cathedral 28
State Library 23
Stawell 87
Stratford 44
Sturt Street 80
Surf Lifesaving Clubs 116
Symbols 7

T

Taxis 15
Telecommunications Tower 59
Telephones 115
Television 116
Time Zones 116
Tisdall Winery 72
Tocumwal 60
Tollways 15
Toolangi 47
Torquay 106
Tourism Victoria 10
Tower Hill State Game Reserve 98
Train ticket prices 118
Train travel 118
Trams 14
Travel Information 117
  Accommodation 117
  How To Get to Australia 117
  Travelling to and around Queensland 119
  Travelling Within Australia 118
Travelling to and around Queensland 119
Travelling Within Australia 118
Treasury Gardens 27
Treasury, Old 26
Trip Log 130
Tuki Fishing Complex 81
Twelve Apostles 101
Tynong 35

u

University of Melbourne 30

v

Victoria Park Lake 59
Victoria Visitor Information Centre 10
Victoria: An Overview 111
Victorian Alps 49
Victorian Arts Centre Complex 27
Victorian Tourism Operators Association 10
Victoria's Farm Shed 35
Videos 116
View Street 66
Vintage Talking Trams 66
Violet Town 61
Virgin Blue 118
Visa 116

w

Walks around Bright 51
Wannon Falls 110
Warrnambool 95
  Accommodation 96
  Characteristics 95
  Climate 95
  Eating Out 97
  Facilities 98
  Festivals 98
  How to Get There 95
  Outlying Attractions 99
  Points of Interest 97
  Tours 98
  Visitor Information 97
Warrnambool Art Gallery 98
Warrnambool Botanic Gardens 98
Wentworth 94
William Ricketts Sanctuary 36
Wineries around Ballarat 82
Wineries around Mildura 94
Woodsie's Gem Shop 92
World in Wax Museum 71

y

Yarra Glen 47
Yarra Valley 45
Yarra Valley Expo 48
Young & Jackson's Hotel 28

Index

Budget Form

This form will help you to plan your Victorian trip.

Area of Victoria:		
Basic Distance:		km
Side Trips, etc. (allow 10%):		km
Connecting Route Distance:		km
Total Distance:		km

TOWN	Distance	Fuel	Car Service	Accomm.	Food	Fees, Charges	Other Expenses
TOTAL							
GRAND TOTAL =							

NOTES:

Budget Form

This form will help you to plan your Victorian trip.

Area of Victoria:	
Basic Distance:	km
Side Trips, etc. (allow 10%):	km
Connecting Route Distance:	km
Total Distance:	km

TOWN	Distance	Fuel	Car Service	Accomm.	Food	Fees, Charges	Other Expenses
TOTAL							
GRAND TOTAL =							

NOTES:

Trip Log

List your expenditures here.

Date	Town	Speedo	Fuel $	Accom $	Meals $	Other Expenses $
	TOTALS=					

Photo Log

Roll 1	Roll 2	Roll 3
1	1	1
2	2	2
3	3	3
4	4	4
5	5	5
6	6	6
7	7	7
8	8	8
9	9	9
10	10	10
11	11	11
12	12	12
13	13	13
14	14	14
15	15	15
16	16	16
17	17	17
18	18	18
19	19	19
20	20	20
21	21	21
22	22	22
23	23	23
24	24	24
25	25	25
26	26	26
27	27	27
28	28	28
29	29	29
30	30	30
31	31	31
32	32	32
33	33	33
34	34	34
35	35	35
36	36	36

Maps Index

Ararat and the Grampians 84
Australia's East 6
Australia's East (opposite) 192
Ballarat 76
Bendigo Region 65
Bright and the Victorian Alps 50
Echuca-Moama 71
Geelong 105
Healesville and the Yarra Valley 47
Lakes Entrance 41
Melbourne region,
     North and East 8
Melbourne region,
     South and West 9
Melbourne City Map 25
Mildura 91
Portland 109
Shepparton Region 59
Warrnambool and
     the Great Ocean Road 96